JESUS, THE TEMPLE AND THE COMING SON OF MAN

AND THE

ROBERT H. STEIN

A COMMENTARY ON MARK 13

IVP Academic
An imprint of InterVarsity Press
Downers Grove, Illinois

InterVarsity Press
P.O. Box 1400, Downers Grove, IL 60515-1426
World Wide Web: www.ivpress.com
Email: email@ivpress.com

©2014 by Robert H. Stein

All rights reserved. No part of this book may be reproduced in any form without written permission from InterVarsity Press.

InterVarsity Press® is the book-publishing division of InterVarsity Christian Fellowship/USA®, a movement of students and faculty active on campus at hundreds of universities, colleges and schools of nursing in the United States of America, and a member movement of the International Fellowship of Evangelical Students. For information about local and regional activities, write Public Relations Dept., InterVarsity Christian Fellowship/USA, 6400 Schroeder Rd., P.O. Box 7895, Madison, WI 53707-7895, or visit the IVCF website at www.intervarsity.org.

Scripture quotations, unless otherwise noted, are from the New Revised Standard Version of the Bible, copyright 1989 by the Division of Christian Education of the National Council of the Churches of Christ in the USA. Used by permission. All rights reserved.

Cover design: David Fassett
Interior design: Beth McGill
Images: Second Temple: © jscalev/iStockphoto
gold background: © allibee/iStockphoto
St. Michael: St. Michael Weighing the Souls, from the Last Judgement by Rogier van der Weyden at Hotel Dieu, Beaune, France. © Paul Maeyaert. The Bridgeman Art Library

ISBN 978-0-8308-4058-8 (print)
ISBN 978-0-8308-9663-9 (digital)

 As a member of the Green Press Initiative, InterVarsity Press is committed to protecting the environment and to the responsible use of natural resources. To learn more, visit greenpressinitiative.org.

Library of Congress Cataloging-in-Publication Data

Stein, Robert H., 1935-
  Jesus, the temple, and the coming Son of Man : a commentary on Mark 13 / Robert H. Stein.
    pages cm
  Includes bibliographical references and index.
  ISBN 978-0-8308-4058-8 (pbk. : alk. paper)
  1. Bible. Mark XIII—Commentaries. I. Title.
  BS2585.53.S735 2014
  226.3'06—dc23
                            2014022814

| P | 23 | 22 | 21 | 20 | 19 | 18 | 17 | 16 | 15 | 14 | 13 | 12 | 11 | 10 | 9 | 8 | 7 | 6 | 5 | 4 | 3 | 2 | 1 |
| Y | 34 | 33 | 32 | 31 | 30 | 29 | 28 | 27 | 26 | 25 | 24 | 23 | 22 | 21 | 20 | 19 | 18 | 17 | 16 | 15 | 14 |

In appreciation to Bethel University, Bethel Seminary,

and the Southern Baptist Theological Seminary where I have had

the great privilege of teaching for over thirty-five years.

Contents

Outline 9

Abbreviations 11

Preface 15

1 Determining Our Goal 17

2 Key Issues Involved in Interpreting Mark 13 42

3 Jesus' Prediction of the Destruction of
the Temple (and Jerusalem). 50
Mark 13:1-4

4 The Coming Destruction of the Temple (and Jerusalem)
and the Sign Preceding It 70
Mark 13:5-23

5 The Coming of the Son of Man. 103
Mark 13:24-27

6 The Parable of the Fig Tree and the Coming Destruction
of the Temple (and Jerusalem) 121
Mark 13:28-31

7 The Parable of the Watchman and the Exhortation
to Be Alert for the Coming of the Son of Man 128
Mark 13:32-37

8 An Interpretative Translation of Mark 13 136

Bibliography 139

Subject Index 147

Author Index 149

Mark Index 151

Scripture Index 153

Ancient Writings Index 157

Outline

1. **Determining Our Goal**

    Introduction

    Investigating Mark 13 for Information About the Historical Jesus

        The quest for the historical Jesus

        The "new quest" for the historical Jesus

        The "third quest" for the historical Jesus

    Investigating Mark 13 for Information About Its Sources

    Seeking the Meaning of the Evangelist in Writing Mark 13

2. **Key Issues Involved in Interpreting Mark 13**

3. **Jesus' Prediction of the Destruction of the Temple (and Jerusalem): *Mark 13:1-4***

    Text and Introduction

    Mark 13:1: *Jesus Leaves the Temple, and the Disciples Remark About the Temple's Magnificence*

    Mark 13:2: *Jesus Predicts the Temple's Destruction*

    Mark 13:3-4: *The Disciples' Two-Part Question: The Key for Understanding Mark 13*

    Summary

4. **The Coming Destruction of the Temple (and Jerusalem) and the Sign Preceding It: *Mark 13:5-23***

    Text and Introduction

    Mark 13:5-13: *Events That Are Not Signs of the Temple's Imminent Destruction*

        The first non-sign: *The appearance of false messianic claimants (13:5-6)*

        The second non-sign: *The coming of wars and natural disasters (13:7-8)*

        The third non-sign: *The mission and persecution of believers (13:9-13)*

Mark 13:14-20: *The Sign of the Abomination of Desolation Heralding the Temple's and Jerusalem's Imminent Destruction and the Warning to Flee Judea*

Mark 13:21-23: *The Warning of False Messianic Claimants Appearing Shortly Before the Temple's and Jerusalem's Destruction*

Summary

5. The Coming of the Son of Man: *Mark 13:24-27*

    Text and Introduction

    Mark 13:24a: *"But in Those Days, After That Tribulation"*

    Mark 13:24b-25: *The Appearance of Theophanic Signs*

    Mark 13:26-27: *The Coming of the Son of Man*

    Summary

6. The Parable of the Fig Tree and the Coming Destruction of the Temple (and Jerusalem): *Mark 13:28-31*

    Text and Introduction

    Mark 13:28-29: *The Parable of the Fig Tree*

    Mark 13:30-31: *"Truly, I Tell You, This Generation Will Not Pass Away Until..."*

    Summary

7. The Parable of the Watchman and the Exhortation to Be Alert for the Coming of the Son of Man: *Mark 13:32-37*

    Text and Introduction

    Mark 13:32-33: *No One Knows but Only the Father*

    Mark 13:34: *The Parable of the Watchman*

    Mark 13:35-36: *The Application of the Parable to Mark's Readers*

    Mark 13:37: *The Universal Call to Be Prepared for the Parousia of the Son of Man*

8. An Interpretative Translation of Mark 13

Abbreviations

AB	Anchor Bible
ABRL	Anchor Bible Reference Library
AnBib	Analecta Biblica
Ant.	Josephus *Jewish Antiquities*
ANTC	Abington New Testament Commentary
AYB	Anchor Yale Bible
BAR	*Biblical Archeology Review*
BBR	*Bulletin for Biblical Research*
b. B. Meṣ.	The tractate *Babba Meṣiʿa* in the Babylonian Talmud
b. B. Qam.	The tractate *Babba Qamma* in the Babylonian Talmud
b. Ber.	The tractate *Berakot* in the Babylonian Talmud
BECNT	Baker Exegetical Commentary of the New Testament
BETL	Bibliotheca Ephemeridum Theologicorum Lovaniensium
BJRL	*Bulletin of the John Rylands Library*
BNTC	Black New Testament Commentary
CBET	Contributions to Biblical Exegesis and Theology
CBQ	*Catholic Biblical Quarterly*
CBQMS	Catholic Biblical Quarterly Monograph Series
CGTC	Cambridge Greek Testament Commentary
CTJ	*Calvin Theological Journal*
D	The hypothetical material used in the composition of Deuteronomy
E	A group of passages in the Pentateuch in which God is called *Elohim*
EBC	Expositor's Bible Commentary
EKKNT	Evangelisch-katholischer Kommentar zum Neuen Testament
ESV	English Standard Version
FRLANT	Forschungen zur Religion und Literatur des Alten und Neuen Testament

HTKNT	Herder's theologischer Kommentar zum Neuen Testament
HZNT	Handbuch zum Neuen Testament
ICC	International Critical Commentary
J	A group of passages in the Pentateuch in which God is called Yahweh
JBL	*Journal of Biblical Literature*
JSNT	*Journal for the Study of the New Testament*
JSOT	*Journal for the Study of the Old Testament*
JSNTSS	Journal for the Study of the New Testament Supplement Series
JTS	*Journal of Theological Studies*
J.W.	Josephus *Jewish War*
KBANT	Kommentar und Beiträge zum Alten und Neuen Testament
KJV	King James Version
L	Gospel material unique to Luke
LNTS	Library of New Testament Studies
LXX	Septuagint (Greek translation of the Hebrew Old Testament)
M	Gospel material unique to Matthew
NAB	New American Bible
NAC	New American Commentary
NIBC	New International Bible Commentary
NICNT	New International Commentary on the New Testament
NIGTC	New International Greek Testament Commentary
NJB	New Jerusalem Bible
NRSV	New Revised Standard Version
NT	*Novum Testamentum*
NTC	New Testament Commentary
NTL	New Testament Library
NTR	New Testament Readings
NTS	*New Testament Studies*
P	Material in the Pentateuch having special interest in priestly concerns
PGC	Pilgrim Gospel Commentaries
PNTC	Pillar New Testament Commentary
POxy	Oxyrhynchus papyrus

Q	Material common to Matthew and Luke not found in Mark
1QM	The War Scroll in the Dead Sea Scrolls
REB	Revised English Bible
RNT	Regensburger Neuen Testament
RSV	Revised Standard Version
SBLDS	Society of Biblical Literature Dissertation Series
SBT	Studies in Biblical Theology
SNTSMS	Society for New Testament Studies Monograph Series
SP	Sacra Pagina
TENTS	Texts and Editions for New Testament Study
T. Jud.	*Testament of Judah*
T. Naph.	*Testament of Napthali*
WBC	Word Bible Commentary
WTJ	*Westminster Theological Journal*
ZNW	*Zeitschrift für die neutestamentliche Wissenschaft und die Kunde der älteren Kirche*

Preface

My love affair with the Gospel of Mark began when I was a doctoral student at Princeton Theological Seminary and resulted in a dissertation, "The Proper Methodology for Ascertaining a Marcan Redaktionsgeschichte." After graduation it led to the writing of various articles on Mark such as: "The 'Redaktionsgeschichtlich' Investigation of a Mark Seam (Mc 1$^{21\text{ff.}}$)," *ZNW* 61 (1970): 70-94; "The Proper Methodology for Ascertaining a Markan Redaction History," *NT* 13 (1971): 181-98; "A Short Note on Mark XIV.28 and XVI.7," *NTS* 20 (1973): 445-52; "Is the Transfiguration (Mark 9:2-8) a Misplaced Resurrection-Account?" *JBL* 95 (1976): 79-96; "The Matthew-Luke Agreements Against Mark: Insight from John," *CBQ* 54 (1992): 482-502; "The Ending of Mark," *BBR* 18 (2008): 79-88; "Duality in Mark," in *New Studies in the Synoptic Problem: Oxford Conference, April 2008*, ed. P. Foster et al., BETL 239 (2011): 253-80. This interest ultimately culminated in my commentary on Mark in the Baker Exegetical Commentary on the New Testament (2008). That my interest has not waned is evident by the publication of *Jesus, the Temple and the Coming Son of Man*.

For readers who want to know from the very start my thesis of how Mark 13 is best interpreted, I recommend they begin by reading chapter eight, "An Interpretative Translation of Mark 13." For those, however, who would like to work systematically through the problem of how this chapter of Mark is best interpreted, I recommend reading the book beginning with chapter one and continuing consecutively through chapter eight. As in the reading of any mystery novel or thesis, much is lost by not following the progression of the logic and argumentation given.

I want to express my appreciation and gratitude to Dr. Robert L. Plummer of the Southern Baptist Theological Seminary and Dr. Benjamin L. Merkle of Southeastern Baptist Theological Seminary for their careful analysis, suggestions and critique of this work. It was a privilege to have been their teacher and colleague in the study of the New Testament. I also want to thank my sons Keith R. and Stephen W. for their assessment and analysis of the book from the viewpoint of learned laity. Needless to say, whereas numerous positive contributions to this work have come from these men, the final product is my own responsibility. I also want to express my appreciation to Dan Reid and the staff of InterVarsity Press for their assistance in the final editing of this work. It has once again been a privilege to work with them in the publication of this book.

All scriptural quotations found in this book are from the New Revised Standard Version unless otherwise specified.

1

Determining Our Goal

The goal of writing a commentary on Mark 13, sometimes called the "Little Apocalypse" or the "Olivet Discourse," might seem at first glance to be quite obvious. Yet the history of research on this chapter of the Bible reveals that investigators have often had varied and diverse goals in their research. The chapter, the longest continuous series of teachings found in Mark, consists of thirty-nine sentences, compared to the next longest speech of Jesus (8:34-38), which consists of just six sentences.[1] The chapter has proven a rich source mined for numerous subject matters. Some of these are historical in nature and seek to uncover information about the historical Jesus lying behind the present text of Mark. Some are literary in nature and involve the search for hypothetical written and oral sources used in composing the present text. Some involve the investigation of the present, canonical text to discover its authorial meaning. It is clear from this that there is little agreement as to what the goal of writing a commentary on Mark 13 should be.

INVESTIGATING MARK 13 FOR INFORMATION ABOUT THE HISTORICAL JESUS[2]

Most people who read Mark 13 do so in order to learn about what Jesus of Nazareth taught concerning the destruction of the temple and Jerusalem and his second coming. The questions of the disciples in Mark 13:4 ("Tell us, when will this [the destruction of the temple and Jerusalem referred to in 13:2] be, and what will be the sign that all these things are about to be ac-

---

[1] Kenneth Grayston, "The Study of Mark XIII," *BJRL* 56 (1974): 375.
[2] For anyone engaged in a serious study of Mark 13, George R. Beasley-Murray, *Jesus and the Last Days: The Interpretation of the Olivet Discourse* (Peabody, MA: Hendrickson, 1993) serves as a fundamental resource.

complished?") focus the reader's attention on Jesus' answer to them in 13:5-37. The reader faces numerous questions in trying to understand Jesus' answer. Some of these are:

- In 13:6 did Jesus mean that false teachers would come claiming to be him (i.e., Jesus of Nazareth, the risen Christ) or the Jewish messiah longed for by non-Christian Jews?

- Was the prophecy of 13:10 fulfilled already in apostolic times (cf. Paul's statements in Rom 16:26; Col 1:6, 23 that the gospel had become known "to all nations" [RSV]), or does it still await its fulfillment?

- What does Jesus mean by the "abomination of desolation" (ESV) in 13:14, and does his/its appearance involve the events surrounding the fall of Jerusalem in A.D. 70 or the future coming of the Son of Man?

- Is the language of 13:24-27 to be understood literally or figuratively? Is Jesus using this imagery in the same manner as the Old Testament prophets (cf. Is 13:9-11; Jer 4:23-28; Ezek 32:5-8; etc.)—that is, metaphorically?

- Does Jesus teach in 13:24 that his return as the Son of Man would occur immediately after the fall of Jerusalem in 13:14-23?

- What does Jesus mean by "this generation" in 13:30, and was he wrong in his prediction?

- How do Jesus' other sayings on this subject, such as Mark 8:34-38 and Matthew 25:1-46, and the additional comments we find in the parallel accounts (Mt 24:1-51 and Lk 21:5-36) help us understand Jesus' teaching in Mark 13?

A person seeking to ascertain the actual words of Jesus of Nazareth in Mark 13 will soon face an additional series of questions. Simply reading the red-letter words of Mark in an English translation of the Bible will not do, for Jesus did not teach in English! The English language only came into existence by the interaction of the Anglo-Saxon language (a Germanic language that developed among the Angles and Saxons who invaded *Angl*and in the fourth and fifth centuries), French (when the Normans invaded England in the eleventh century) and Latin (due to the influence of the clergy and church). Even if we can read the Greek text of Mark 13, we still face the problem that while Jesus probably knew some first-century Greek (the extent of his knowledge of Greek is debated), his mother tongue was Aramaic, as Mark 5:41; 7:11, 34; 14:36; 15:34; Matthew 5:22, 29; 6:24 indicate. Consequently, the search to understand the specific teachings of the historical Jesus in Mark 13 must ultimately seek to understand the Aramaic words underlying the Greek text of this chapter! Thus the attempt to understand the teachings of Jesus in this chapter involves what has been called "the quest for the historical Jesus" and the pursuit of the *ipsissima verba* (the actual words of Jesus)—or at least his *ipsissima vox* (the voice of Jesus—a more general understanding of what Jesus actually taught)—that lie beneath the present Gospel text.

The quest for the historical Jesus.[3] It is generally agreed that the quest for the historical Jesus began in 1774–1778 when the poet Lessing published Hermann Samuel Reimarus's notes after his death.[4] Originally titled "Fragments from an Unnamed Author," they became known as *The Wolfenbüttel Fragments* because they were found in a library at Wolfenbüttel, Germany.[5] In the *Fragments* Reimarus portrayed the "real" Jesus as one who made no christological claims, instituted no sacraments, and never predicted his death or rose from the dead. He furthermore argued that the Gospel portrayal of Jesus was a deliberate deception of the disciples. Reimarus's work drew an enormous response. Regardless of whether one agreed or disagreed with his statement that "we are justified in drawing an absolute distinction between the teaching of the Apostles in their writings and what Jesus Himself in His own lifetime proclaimed and taught,"[6] the issue of what the Jesus of history was really like and what he actually taught became the focus

---

[3]For a helpful survey of the "quests" for the historical Jesus, see Colin Brown, "Quest of the Historical Jesus," in *Dictionary of Jesus and the Gospels*, rev. ed., ed. Joel B. Green (Downers Grove, IL: IVP Academic, 2013), pp. 718-56.

[4]Although earlier English deists (John Toland, 1670-1722, *Christianity Not Mysterious*; Thomas Woolston, 1669-1732, *Discourses on the Miracles of our Saviour in View of the Present Controversy between Infidels and Apostates*; Matthew Tindal, 1655-1733, *Christianity as Old as the Creation, Or the Gospel, a Republication of the Religion of Nature*) began to doubt various miracles of Jesus in the Gospel accounts, it was Reimarus who first raised these questions and sought to deal with them by means of a historical conception of the life of Jesus.

[5]For an English translation of Reimarus's *Apologie oder Schutzschrift für die vernüftigen Verehrer Gottes*, on which *The Wolfenbüttel Fragments* were based, see Hermann Samuel Reimarus, *Reimarus: Fragments*, ed. Charles H. Talbert, trans. R. S. Fraser, Lives of Jesus (Philadelphia: Fortress, 1970), pp. 59-269.

[6]As quoted in Albert Schweitzer, *The Quest of the Historical Jesus: A Critical Study of Its Progress from Reimarus to Wrede*, trans. W. Montgomery (New York: Macmillan, 1910), p. 16.

of New Testament scholarly discussion. Thus the quest to discover the historical Jesus began, and this would be the focal point of Gospel studies for nearly a century and a half.

The earliest period of this quest involved rationalistic attempts to explain some of the miracles in the Gospels. This was followed by a period in which rationalistic explanations were sought for *all* of the miracles in the Gospels.[7] As time progressed, there developed a gradual loss of confidence in rationalistic attempts to explain the miracle accounts of the life of Jesus found in the Gospels. Meanwhile the influence of David F. Strauss's *Das Leben Jesu* (1835) became increasingly prominent.[8] Strauss argued that one could not arrive at the historical Jesus by rationalizing the miracle accounts, because these accounts were myths and symbolic expressions of general religious truths, not historical sources for the life of Jesus of Nazareth. One should therefore not seek to find some historical kernel concerning the historical Jesus in these myths, but rather "demythologize" them and find the general religious truth contained in them. That religious truth, of course, would cohere with the evolutionary, liberal theology of the day.

This early quest for the historical Jesus had mixed results, to say the least. This is especially true with regard to Jesus' life and actions. Many "questers" brought with them into their investigation of the Gospels the presupposition of a closed universe in which miracles are not possible. The predetermined result was obvious—the Jesus of history worked no miracles and did not experience a resurrection from the dead. The teachings of Jesus fared somewhat better, but the teachings involving the prediction of his death and resurrection; his claims that he could forgive sins, that he had authority over the Old Testament law and that he was the Christ, the Son of Man and the Son of God; and his eschatological teachings were denied authenticity. Often his teachings, especially those involving eschatology, were rejected as inauthentic because of the tastes and values of the researcher. Critical scholars of the eighteenth and nineteenth centuries in general disliked Jesus' eschatological teachings and either radically reinterpreted them (the coming of

---

[7]A good example of this is Heinrich E. G. Paulus, *Das Leben Jesu als Grundlage einer reinen Geschichte des Urchristentums* (Heidelberg: C. F. Winter, 1828).

[8]The English translation of this work, *The Life of Jesus Critically Examined*, trans. George Eliot (London: Chapman), appeared in 1846.

the Son of Man became a symbolic representation of the triumph of the kingdom of God in human hearts), rejected their authenticity (such half-insane imagination could not have come from such a great teacher as Jesus but represented corrupt Jewish religion), or saw them as the remnants of Jesus' primitive Jewish heritage. Such views were especially prominent among German scholars.[9] Thus the authenticity or inauthenticity of the teachings of Jesus found in the Gospels were frequently judged by the beliefs and values of their researchers. Those that coincided with the ideals of progressive, liberal thinking or could be reinterpreted to teach them were deemed authentic; those that did not were considered primitive and unworthy of nineteenth-century, enlightenment thinking and thus were deemed inauthentic.

At the end of the nineteenth and the beginning of the twentieth century several devastating criticisms of the quest for the historical Jesus arose that caused its "death." One of these was Martin Kähler's *The So-Called Historical Jesus and the Historic Biblical Christ* (1892).[10] In this work Kähler demonstrated that it was not the so-called historical Jesus of the questers who had exercised an influence in history and with whom millions had communed in childlike faith, but the Christ who is proclaimed and found in the Gospels.[11] This realization both destroyed the motivation of the quest and indicated that theologically it was illegitimate, for the Jesus of the "quest" had no essential connection with the Christ of faith. Another work that had a crushing effect on the quest was William Wrede's *Das Messiasgeheimnis in den Evangelien* (1901).[12] Wrede demonstrated that Mark, which was thought to be the earliest of the Gospels and therefore the most untainted by early Christian modification, was not in fact a neutral and objective report of the life of the his-

---

[9]Does the description of Jewish eschatological and messianic hopes as primitive, fanatic, corrupt, Jewish religion reflect anti-Semitism on the part of many of the questers in nineteenth-century Germany? Under the Nazis such anti-Semitism became blatant, as in the case of Walter Grundmann, *Jesus der Galiläer und das Judentum* (Leipzig: Wigand, 1940).

[10]The English translation of this work by Carl E. Braaten was published by Fortress Press in Philadelphia in 1964. The original German version is titled *Der sogenannte historische Jesus und der geschichtliche, biblische Christus* (Leipzig: A. Deichert, 1892).

[11]Martin Kähler, *The So-Called Historical Jesus and the Historic Biblical Christ*, trans. Carl E. Braaten (Philadelphia: Fortress, 1964), p. 66.

[12]This was published in Göttingen by Vandenhoeck & Ruprecht. The English translation, *The Messianic Secret*, trans. J. C. G. Greig (Cambridge: James Clarke), surprisingly did not appear until 1971.

torical Jesus. On the contrary, it was written in faith for faith.[13] The rise of form criticism at the end of World War I further demonstrated that before our Gospels were written the Gospel traditions were transmitted orally and that their preservation and shaping were determined by the religious concerns of the early church. This shattered the confidence of the questers as to whether it was possible to recover the real, historical Jesus, because of the religious commitment of the transmitters of the Jesus tradition. A third major blow to historical Jesus research was Albert Schweitzer's *The Quest of the Historical Jesus* (1906).[14] In this work Schweitzer demonstrated that the resultant "historical" Jesus of the quest was the creation of liberalism and made in the image of liberal researchers.[15] The real Jesus, Schweitzer pointed out, was in reality an offense to liberalism. He was not a nineteenth-century, liberal prophet with the Enlightenment views and values of nineteenth-century questers but was instead a first-century Jewish prophet looking forward to and proclaiming an eschatological event—the coming of the kingdom of God and the arrival of the Son of Man from heaven.[16] Schweitzer's criticism of the quest for the historical Jesus was convincing and devastating. Liberal questers quickly realized that the result of any real quest for the historical Jesus would result in an eschatological Jesus whose teachings and actions were an affront and offense to their theological liberalism. Schweitzer's work dealt a death blow to the quest and destroyed the motivation for it.

---

[13]Compare Günther Bornkamm's *Jesus of Nazareth*, trans. I. McLusky et al. (New York: Harper, 1960), the most famous "life of Jesus" produced by the later "new quest" of the historical Jesus: "We possess no single word of Jesus and no single story of Jesus, no matter how incontestably genuine they may be, which do not contain at the same time the confession of the believing congregation or at least are embedded therein. This makes the search after the bare facts of history difficult and to a large extend futile" (p. 14).

[14]The German title is *Von Reimarus zu Wrede: eine Geschichte der Leben-Jesu-Forschung* (Tübingen: Mohr Siebeck, 1906). The English translation appeared in 1910.

[15]In his concluding chapter titled "Results," Schweitzer, *Quest*, p. 398, states: "The Jesus of Nazareth who came forward publicly as the Messiah, who preached the ethic of the Kingdom of God, who founded the Kingdom of Heaven upon earth, and died to give His work its final consecration, never had any existence. He is a figure designed by rationalism, endowed with life by liberalism, and clothed by modern theology in an historical garb." Cf. also George Tyrrell, *Christianity at the Cross-Roads* (New York: Longmans, 1910), p. 44: "The Christ that Harnack [and other questers] see, looking back through nineteen centuries of Catholic darkness, is only the reflection of a Liberal Protestant face, seen at the bottom of a deep well."

[16]Schweitzer, *Quest*, pp. 398-99, states that the real Jesus "will not be a Jesus Christ to whom the religion of the present [the theological liberalism of the nineteenth century] can ascribe, according to its long-cherished custom, its own thoughts and ideas, as it did with the Jesus of its own making.... The historical Jesus will be to our time a stranger and an enigma."

A fourth reason for the death of the quest of the historical Jesus was the recognition of the subjective element involved in historical research. The leading historian of the nineteenth century was Leopold von Ranke (1797–1886). Von Ranke sought to base historical investigation on genuine and original documents, in order to understand *wie es eigentlich gewesen*—that is, simply to know how it really was. He based his research on sources such as diaries, memoirs, firsthand eyewitness accounts, diplomatic dispatches and government documents (such as the Venetian archives), and so on. Thus he is rightly recognized as the founder of source-based historiography. However, toward the end of the nineteenth century historians began to recognize the subjective element involved in all historical research. Wilhelm Dilthey (1833–1911) in particular demonstrated that there was no such thing as objective, presuppositionless historiography. In his "critique on historical reason" he pointed out that all historical research is interpreted history, for historical facts do not simply speak for themselves. They must be interpreted. The historian must determine which "facts" of history should be investigated, and this choice involves their significance for the investigator.[17] The recognition of the subjective element in historical research and the role of historians' presuppositions in their research destroyed confidence in whether a truly, objective quest of the historical Jesus was possible. The result of these developments in New Testament studies was the death of the "old" quest for the historical Jesus.

The "new quest" for the historical Jesus.[18] From 1918 to 1953 the quest for the historical Jesus lay for the most part dormant. This disinterest in the Jesus of history was especially true in Germany. Scriptural support for this was sought in Paul's apparent disinterest in the historical Jesus in 2 Corinthians 5:16, where he says, "From now on, therefore, we regard no one according to the flesh. Even though we once regarded Christ according to the

---

[17]Cf. ibid, p. 4: "The historical investigation of the life of Jesus did not take its rise from a purely historical interest; it turned to the Jesus of history as an ally in the struggle against the tyranny of [Christian] dogma." Note also the conclusion of N. T. Wright in *Jesus and the Victory of God* (Minneapolis: Fortress, 1996), p. 17: "The 'Quest' began as an explicitly anti-theological, anti-Christian, anti-dogmatic movement. Its initial agenda was *not* [his italics] to find a Jesus upon whom Christian faith might be based, but to show that the faith of the church (as it was then conceived) could not in fact be based on the real Jesus of Nazareth."

[18]The title for this new stage in Jesus research came from James M. Robinson, *A New Quest for the Historical Jesus and Other Essays,* SBT 15 (London: SCM Press, 1959).

flesh, we regard him thus no longer" (ESV).[19] This attitude changed in 1953 when Ernst Käsemann delivered an address that was published the next year.[20] In it he pointed out that scholars could not simply ignore the Jesus of history, for to do so would be to fall into the error of docetism, an early Christian heresy which denied the true humanity of Jesus of Nazareth. He also pointed out that as true historians scholars had to acknowledge that they possessed in the Gospels authentic material concerning the life and teachings of the historical Jesus.[21] He then described a tool or criterion to investigate the Gospel materials—if we find material in the Gospels that could not have been derived from Judaism or primitive Christianity, especially when Jewish Christianity has mitigated or modified it, it can confidently be assumed to be authentic.[22] (See the discussion of the criteria of *dissimilarity* and *embarrassment* below.)

Käsemann's appeal for a new quest and his suggested criterion received a receptive response. Scholars enthusiastically took up the challenge, and the "new quest for the historical Jesus" became a focus of much New Testament research. Whereas the original quest sought to demonstrate a discontinuity between the Jesus of history and the Jesus of faith found in the Gospels and thus separate the Christian kerygma from the historical Jesus, the new quest sought to demonstrate a continuity between the Christ of the

---

[19]The interpretation of this verse as indicating disinterest on the part of Paul concerning the Jesus of history is based on a misinterpretation. "According to the flesh" (*kata sarka*) is best understood as an adverbial clause modifying the verb *regarded* rather than as an adjectival clause modifying the noun *Christ*. Paul here rejects his former, pre-Christian understanding of Jesus that was "according to the flesh" (cf. Rom 7:7-25). He does not reject the Christ "according to the flesh," i.e., the historical Jesus.

[20]Käsemann's original article was titled "Das Problem des Historischen Jesus" and appeared in *Zeitschrift für Theologie und Kirche* 51 (1954): 125-53. An English translation is found in Ernst Käsemann, "The Problem of the Historical Jesus," in *Essays on New Testament Themes*, trans. W. J. Montague, SBT 41 (London: SCM Press, 1964), pp. 15-47.

[21]"We should . . . be overlooking the fact there are still pieces of the Synoptic tradition which the historian has to acknowledge as authentic if he wishes to remain an historian at all" (Käsemann, "Problem of the Historical Jesus," p. 46). Cf. also Robinson, *New Quest*, p. 76: "A new quest must be built upon the fact that the sources *do* make possible a new kind of quest working in terms of the modern view of history and the self."

[22]Käsemann, "Problem of the Historical Jesus," p. 37. Käsemann here is essentially repeating the tool suggested by his teacher. See Rudolf Bultmann, *The History of the Synoptic Tradition*, trans. John Marsh (New York: Harper, 1963), p. 205: "We can only count on possessing a genuine similitude of Jesus where, on the one hand, expression is given to the contrast between Jewish morality and piety, and the distinctive eschatological temper which characterized the preaching of Jesus; and where on the other hand we find no specifically Christian features."

kerygma and the historical Jesus. Because the new questers for the most part assumed the same naturalistic understanding of the universe as the old questers—that is, they denied the possibility of miracles—the continuity sought did not involve such issues as Jesus' miracles, his resurrection from the dead or his future coming. Instead they sought to demonstrate continuity between the call to decision and existential encounter in the teachings of Jesus and the offer of authentic existence in the proclamation of the early church.[23] A problem soon became evident. The Gospels and the church proclaim that Jesus is the Christ and Son of God; that he died for the sins of the world, rose triumphantly from the dead and ascended into heaven; and that he will return one day in vindication as the Son of Man to judge the world. The questers, both old and new, had for the most part claimed that such material in the Gospels was inauthentic and unworthy of Jesus. The inadequacy of the new quest's search for establishing a significant continuity between the Jesus of history and the proclaimed Christ of the Gospels soon became clear.[24]

The more lasting result of the new quest was to once again raise interest in historical Jesus studies. Scholars, inspired by Käsemann, sought to find various "criteria of authenticity" by which they could establish more objectively the authenticity of various sayings of Jesus. Some of these criteria that have proved especially helpful are:

1. *Multiple attestation.* This criterion assumes that the greater the number of witnesses attesting a teaching of Jesus, the greater the probability is of it being authentic. These witnesses are Mark, Q (the material common to Matthew and Luke not found in Mark), M (the material unique to Matthew), L (the material unique to Luke) and John.

2. *Multiple forms.* This criterion assumes that if a particular teaching of Jesus is found in multiple literary forms, it is more likely to be authentic. Thus the fact that Jesus' teaching on the arrival of the kingdom of God

---

[23]Just as the first questers approached their quest for the historical Jesus from the perspective of the theological liberalism of the eighteenth and nineteenth centuries, so the new questers approached their quest from the perspective of the philosophical existentialism of the first half of the twentieth century.

[24]It should be noted that the best-known attempt at a life of Jesus during the new quest, Bornkamm's *Jesus of Nazareth*, states at the very beginning, "No one is any longer in the position to write a life of Jesus" (p. 13).

in his ministry is found in parables, miracle stories, various sayings and stories about Jesus argues for its authenticity.

3. *Aramaic linguistic phenomena.* Since Jesus' native tongue was Aramaic, the presence of Aramaic terms and of customs of Aramaic-speaking Jews in Palestine, such as the avoidance of God's name by the use of the "divine passive" (a passive tense allows the avoidance of the mention of God as the subject of the action),[25] as well as the substitution of another term for God (e.g., "kingdom of *heaven*"),[26] suggests that in such cases we may well be dealing with a saying or custom that reflects the situation of Jesus.

4. *Dissimilarity.* This criterion argues that if a saying of Jesus conflicts with the teachings of Judaism in Jesus' day and the teachings of the early church, it almost assuredly is authentic. This criterion was hailed with great fanfare as a sure indicator of Jesus' teaching and is quite useful, but it is, however, also quite limited in its applicability. A Jesus who taught nothing in common with the Judaism of his day and the teachings of the early church would be a startling anachronism. Thus while this criterion is quite helpful in detecting what is distinctive in Jesus' teachings, it is not particularly helpful in detecting what is characteristic, and it is the latter that is more important.[27]

5. *Embarrassment.* This criterion assumes that a saying or action of Jesus that would have embarrassed the believing community (such as Jesus submitting to John the Baptist's baptism of repentance, Mk 1:4, 9; cf. Mt 3:13-17, or Jesus' confession that he was ignorant of the day or hour of the end, Mk 13:32) almost certainly must be authentic. It is highly unlikely that someone in the Christian church would have created such embarrassing traditions.

6. *Tradition contrary to editorial tendency.* When we find sayings or actions of Jesus that are contrary to an Evangelist's emphases, it indicates that

---

[25]Examples of the use of the divine passive to avoid the use of God's name can be found in Mt 7:1, 7; 10:30; Mk 4:25; 10:40.

[26]Examples of the use of substitution or circumlocution to avoid God's name can be found in Mt 5:34-35; 6:9; Mk 11:30; 14:61-62; Lk 6:35; 12:8-9; 15:10, 21.

[27]For a helpful survey of the use and development of this criterion, see Gerd Theissen and Dagmar Winter, *The Quest for the Plausible Jesus: The Question of Criteria*, trans. M. Eugene Boring (Louisville: Westminster John Knox, 2002).

such a tradition was so well-known and established that it was included by the Evangelist in his Gospel despite his own editorial purposes in writing. Such a well-known tradition is likely to be authentic. (Contrast Mt 11:13 with the strong Matthean emphasis on the permanence of the law found in his Gospel.)

7. *Eschatological character of sayings.* Unlike the old questers who rejected the authenticity of Jesus' eschatological teachings found in the Gospels, scholars now recognize that Jesus' teachings are thoroughly eschatological in nature. This criterion is most helpful in preventing scholars from modernizing Jesus and making him in our own image. The similarity of Jesus' teachings with first-century Jewish eschatological thinking is now recognized not as a negative factor but a positive one in judging their authenticity. Jesus' teaching differed in various aspects with contemporary Jewish thinking in the first century, but it was not that his thinking was noneschatological as the nineteenth-century questers maintained! His teachings were thoroughly eschatological and centered on his pronouncement that the kingdom of God had arrived.[28]

8. *Parables and poetry.* It is quite evident that Jesus made great use of these literary forms. Even the more critical scholars acknowledge that in these literary forms found in the Gospels we are at the bedrock of the Jesus traditions. On the other hand, these literary forms are rarely found in the teachings of the early church (this is especially true with respect to the parables), so we should come with a positive attitude toward the authenticity of this kind of material in the Gospels.[29]

9. *Coherence or consistency.* Once we arrive at a general understanding of Jesus' teachings and at a critically assured minimum, other teachings of Jesus in the Gospels that fit this minimum should probably be considered authentic and the burden of proof placed on attempts to deny their authenticity.

---

[28]It is interesting to note that, whereas in the nineteenth century the eschatological teachings of Jesus were considered inauthentic because they resembled Jewish messianic and apocalyptic hopes, now the presence of such features is generally seen as a sign of their authenticity!

[29]Cf. the following statement from Klyne R. Snodgrass, "Parable," in *Dictionary of Jesus and the Gospels*, ed. Joel B. Green and Scot McKnight (Downers Grove, IL: InterVarsity Press, 1992), p. 596: "Even scholars who are persuaded that the Gospel parables include additions by the early church still view the parables as providing some of the most authentic and reliable teaching from Jesus."

Certain criteria have also been found that serve a negative function in the pursuit of the authentic teachings of Jesus. Some of these are:

1. *The tendencies of the developing tradition.* During the early days of form criticism, there was great confidence that the passing on of oral tradition followed certain laws and that by knowing these laws we could apply them to the Gospel traditions to arrive at earlier forms of the tradition. These laws were determined by noting how Matthew and Luke used Mark, how the later apocryphal Gospels used the canonical Gospels and how folk traditions developed in various cultures over the centuries. Knowing these "laws" of tradition development, we could apply them in reverse to the present Gospel traditions, remove later church crustaceans and arrive at their earlier, more primitive forms. Later, more careful investigation, however, found that these supposed "laws" were not laws at all, and that many times these "tendencies" were found to have comparable countertendencies. (Sometimes we find that the later form of a tradition tends to be more specific, such as giving the names of people involved; sometimes we find the later form of the tradition tends to be less specific and more general.)[30] Furthermore, the short time between the ministry of Jesus and the writing of the Gospels argues against the development of these tendencies, which in many of the examples used took place over hundreds of years. The presence of the eyewitnesses (Lk 1:2) also placed a damper on any radical modification of what was considered "sacred" tradition (Mk 8:34-38; 13:31).

2. *Environmental and linguistic contradiction.* It is essentially an axiom that a saying or action that violates the environmental and literary world of Jesus cannot be authentic—that is, a saying of Jesus that he *could not* have said in his ministry he *did not* say. (The saying in the *Gospel of Thomas* 47, "It is impossible for a man to ride two horses," might be authentic, but a saying such as "It is impossible for a man to ride two motorcycles" could not be.) It is often argued that Mark 10:11-12 is not authentic with respect to a woman divorcing her husband, because this

---

[30]E. P. Sanders, *The Tendencies of the Synoptic Tradition*, SNTSMS 9 (New York: Cambridge University Press, 1969) is most helpful in this respect. He concludes, "*Dogmatic statements that a certain characteristic proves a certain passage to be earlier than another are never justified*" (p. 272, his italics).

was not permitted in Jewish law. But a letter written during the Bar Kokhba revolt (A.D. 132-35) refers to a woman divorcing her husband, and more importantly we should remember that John the Baptist, the cousin of Jesus, was beheaded for saying essentially the same thing Jesus says in Mark 10:12 (cf. Mk 6:17-29).

3. *Contradiction of authentic sayings.* Even as teachings attributed to Jesus in the Gospels that are in harmony with the generally accepted authentic sayings of Jesus are more likely to be authentic, so teachings that contradict such sayings are more likely to be inauthentic. Care must be taken, however, in determining if a saying of Jesus found in the Gospels really contradicts other sayings. The present writer has often found that many such alleged contradictions do not take sufficient note of Jesus' use of hyperbole and exaggeration as literary forms, as well as his use of poetry and puns and the context in which they occur.

Along with these criteria dealing with the authenticity or inauthenticity of individual sayings or teachings in the Gospels, there are several factors that shape one's general attitude toward the reliability of written sources. These involve the age of the tradition, the local coloring of the tradition and the independence of various traditions.[31]

The search for the actual words of Jesus has had mixed results, and for critical scholars the burden of proof is placed on the argument that the sayings of Jesus found in the Gospels are authentic. This is an unwarranted skepticism that assumes the Gospel accounts are guilty (unreliable) unless proven innocent (reliable). The use of the criteria for authenticity should not be understood as seeking to prove the innocence (reliability) of certain Gospel sayings but rather as providing additional evidence for the authenticity of various sayings in the Gospels.[32]

During the last quarter of the twentieth century one manifestation of the

---

[31]See Theissen and Winter, *Quest for the Plausible Jesus*, pp. 12-15.
[32]For a more detailed discussion of the criteria for authenticity, see Robert H. Stein, "The 'Criteria' for Authenticity," in *Gospel Perspectives: Studies of History and Tradition in the Four Gospels*, ed. R. T. France and David Wenham (Sheffield: JSOT Press, 1980), pp. 225-63; Stanley E. Porter, *The Criteria for Authenticity in Historical-Jesus Research: Previous Discussions and New Proposals*, JSNTSS 191 (Sheffield: Sheffield Academic Press, 2000); Theissen and Winter, *Quest for the Plausible Jesus*.

"new quest" was the Jesus Seminar,[33] a group of scholars in North America who investigated the Jesus materials, both canonical and extracanonical (the most important of the latter being the *Gospel of Thomas*), and sought to determine the degree of authenticity of the sayings and actions of Jesus found in these materials. Authenticity would be determined by the vote of the seminar members in which colored beads revealed the degree of probability the voters attributed to a saying or action being authentic. A red bead denoted that the voter thought that the saying was authentic; a pink bead meant that they thought the saying was probably authentic; a gray bead denoted that it was thought probably inauthentic; a black bead that it was considered inauthentic. The result of the voting can be found in *The Five Gospels*.[34]

In practice the method of weighing ballots at times brought questionable results. For example, if a majority voted red or pink—that is, a saying was seen as authentic or probably authentic—but a high proportion of the minority voted black, the result could be a gray rating—that is, probably inauthentic. Such a result is highly dubious. In addition, it should be noted that there was present among many of the scholars a strong antieschatological bias, just as in the original questers. This is evident in the resultant coloring of Mark 13. The entire chapter is either black or gray, and the predominant color is black, with only 13:2, 21, 28-29, 32, 34-36 being gray. With respect to Matthew 24–25, both chapters are either black or gray with only Matthew 25:14-28 being pink.

It is fair to say that the group that made up the Jesus Seminar was far from being representative of New Testament scholars worldwide. It was made up almost exclusively of North American scholars, and even here there was a disproportionate representation of the theological left wing of New Testament scholarship. The degree of credence give to extrabiblical sources such as the *Gospel of Thomas* (note the title, *The Five Gospels*) and to such hypothetical sources such as the *Secret Gospel of Mark* and the *Cross Gospel* is totally unwarranted. Some seminar members even valued the *Gospel of Thomas* more highly than our canonical Gospels. This may be due to the minimization of eschatology in the *Gospel of Thomas*, which concurs with

---

[33]Although some argue that the Jesus Seminar belongs more properly to the "third quest," it contrasts greatly with the very Jewish Jesus of that quest.

[34]Robert W. Funk and Roy W. Hoover, *The Five Gospels: The Search for the Authentic Words of Jesus* (New York: Poleridge, 1993).

the same antieschatological bias possessed by the earliest questers. As to the dating of the *Gospel of Thomas*, some seminar members placed it as having been written in the 50s before any of the canonical Gospels. In contrast most scholars date it around A.D. 180.[35]

With respect to the *Secret Gospel of Mark*, supposedly discovered in 1958 by Morton Smith,[36] for years the only access to it has been a set of black-and-white photographs of the text contained in a book published by Smith in 1973. In 2000 color photographs of the manuscript were published. At present the whereabouts of the actual manuscript is unknown, so that access to it is only available by these two sets of photographs. There is great debate as to whether the *Secret Gospel of Mark* is a fraudulent hoax, perhaps perpetrated by Smith himself, or is "authentic" in the sense that it was written by someone in the eighteenth century who was copying an earlier second-century work. Although some scholars believe that the *Secret Gospel of Mark* was written before our canonical Gospels and served as a source for the Gospel of Mark, very few hold this position. As of 2013 the manuscript's whereabouts are unknown, and thus the ink and fiber of the alleged manuscript have never been subjected to examination. As a result—unless access to the manuscript becomes available and it is subjected to exacting scientific investigation and passes such tests—the *Secret Gospel of Mark* cannot be taken seriously as a source of information concerning either the origin of the Gospel of Mark or the historical Jesus.

The *Cross Gospel*, which some Jesus Seminar members argue is earlier than the canonical Gospels, has a similar history. It is allegedly part of a second-century work called the *Gospel of Peter*, referred to by Eusebius (260-340), the famous early church historian. In 1886-1887 a codex was discovered at Akhamin, Egypt, that is generally assumed to contain a fragment of this Gospel. Within the *Gospel of Peter* several scholars claim to have discovered an old tradition, a "Cross Gospel," that served as a source for the writers of the canonical Gospels. Additional fragments of the *Gospel*

---

[35]See Craig A. Evans, *Fabricating Jesus: How Modern Scholars Distort the Gospels* (Downers Grove, IL: InterVarsity Press, 2006), pp. 52-77.

[36]The actual fragment of the *Secret Gospel of Mark* is found in a manuscript claiming to be an unknown letter of Clement of Alexandria. It appears in some end papers of a seventeenth-century printed collection of the works of Ignatius of Antioch. It is written in Greek in an eighteenth-century hand.

of Peter (POxy 2949 and 4009) were found in the 1970s and 80s. To argue that this material, dealing with the crucifixion and resurrection of Jesus (hence the *Cross Gospel*), is earlier and more authentic than the corresponding material in the canonical Gospels is unconvincing. The accounts—which refer to the scribes, Pharisees and elders confessing Jesus' righteousness; a moving cross that talks; the "Lord's Day"; the presence of angels whose heads extend above the heavens; and so on—give little support for it being considered as providing an earlier and more reliable, historical source than our canonical Gospels, no matter how much it is surgically pruned of secondary materials. Thus the claim that these extracanonical materials are supposedly more primitive and authentic sources for arriving at the real Jesus disappears under closer scrutiny, as surely as the morning haze vanishes at the appearance of the coming midday sun.[37]

The "third quest" for the historical Jesus.[38] In contrast to the Jesus Seminar, which "de-Judaized" and "de-eschatologized" Jesus and in many ways continued the pursuit of the old questers, the "third quest" promises a more lasting achievement. This is because it is based on a more sound foundation: the full recognition of the Jewish origin and character of the historical Jesus and the eschatological nature of his ministry and teaching.[39] Here, ironically in contrast to the Jesus Seminar and the old questers, Jewish and eschatological features in the Gospel accounts are seen as evidence of their authenticity not inauthenticity. The third quest added an important criterion to those already suggested: "double similarity." If a saying of Jesus appears credible (though perhaps deeply subversive) within the Judaism of the first century, and it appears credible as a starting point (though not the exact replica) of later Christian teaching, this "double similarity" argues for its authenticity.[40]

---

[37]For a more detailed discussion and critique, see Evans, *Fabricating Jesus*, pp. 78-99.
[38]The designation "the 'third quest' of the historical Jesus" comes from N. T. Wright, in Stephen Neill and Tom Wright, *The Interpretation of the New Testament 1861-1986*, 2nd ed. (New York: Oxford University Press, 1988), p. 379.
[39]See John P. Meier, "The Present State of the 'Third Quest' for the Historical Jesus: Loss and Gain," *Biblica* 80 (1999), pp. 485-87; cf. also Martin Hengel, "Tasks of New Testament Scholarship," *BBR* 6 (1996), p. 70: "Today one may say that among the most important insights of our field of study [New Testament] since the Second World War belongs the recognition of how deeply rooted earliest Christianity is in Judaism as its native soil."
[40]N. T. Wright, *Jesus and the Victory of God* (Minneapolis: Fortress, 1997), p. 132.

Determining Our Goal 33

The investigation of Mark 13 for Jesus' teachings about the destruction of the temple, the fall of Jerusalem and the coming of the Son of Man is a legitimate and worthwhile task. It is, however, not as simple as may be thought at first, as the difficulties noted above indicate. One additional difficulty that needs to be mentioned is the probability, acknowledged by most scholars, that the sayings of Jesus in Mark 13 were not all proclaimed at the same time and in the same order. If, as is probable, some were taught by Jesus at different times, the order and the logical progression of the argument in 13:5-37 is not so much that of Jesus as that of Mark. Nevertheless it appears reasonable to conclude that the Jesus of Mark 13 taught the following:

- The temple and city of Jerusalem would be destroyed in the lifetime of the disciples.
- Wars, natural disasters, false prophets and messianic pretenders would arise, but these were neither signs nor immediate precursors of the temple's destruction but part of the natural order of things.
- The followers of Jesus would face persecution and, either through or despite this, spread the gospel to all nations.
- In their persecution the Holy Spirit would be with them and aid them in their defense.
- An "abomination of desolation" would precede Jerusalem's destruction, and the believing community should take this as a sign to flee the city immediately.
- The Son of Man would come from heaven and gather his elect from throughout the world.
- No one knows the time of his return but God alone, and as a result believers should live a life prepared for his arrival.

We will look at the exegetical basis for these conclusions in chapters three to seven below.

INVESTIGATING MARK 13 FOR INFORMATION ABOUT ITS SOURCES

During the nineteenth century the search for written sources used in the writing of the biblical accounts played a dominant role in the investigation of the Pentateuch and the Synoptic Gospels. For the Pentateuch this involved sources referred to as J (a group of passages in which God is called *Yahweh* [the "J" comes from the German spelling of the name]), E (a group of passages in which God is called *Elohim*), P (a group of passages having special interest in priestly matters) and D (material that was used in the writing of the book of Deuteronomy). With respect to the Synoptic Gospels the basic sources are understood as Mark (our present Mark, although some scholars argued for the existence of a Proto-Mark that was different from but the basic source of the canonical Mark), Q (the common material found in Matthew and Luke but not in Mark), M (the material unique to Matthew) and L (the material unique to Luke). Some scholars argue for the existence of a Proto-Luke that was essentially an early version of Luke, but this is not generally accepted. It is also believed that before the present canonical Gospels were written, the gospel traditions contained in them were passed on orally. These existed both as individual pieces of tradition and as collections of parables, miracle stories, pronouncement stories, a passion narrative, a birth narrative and so on. Some of these collections were probably also written down. Exactly how this material was used by Mark, the earliest Gospel writer, is, however, far from certain.

Proportionally more time and effort have been spent on the source analysis of Mark 13 than on any similarly sized portion of the Bible. The work that had the most to do with commencing the search for the sources of Mark 13 is T. Coloni's *Jésus Christ et les croyances messianiques de son Temps,* which appeared in 1864. This work was based on Coloni's earlier works and conclusions that Jesus avoided the application of the title "Messiah" to himself, only considered himself a prophet, and preached that the kingdom of God had already come and would gradually extend over all humanity. Thus Jesus did not believe that he would come as the Son of Man in any apocalyptic manner to bring the kingdom of God. Coloni also believed that such statements as Mark 13:24-27 in which the Son of Man returns soon after the fall of Jerusalem, and 13:30 in which the end of history would take place within the lifetime of the disciples, were not authentic teachings of Jesus because Jesus could not have been so mistaken on such things. It was the disciples who later added such Jewish messianic and apocalyptic beliefs to the Jesus traditions. In his study of Mark 13 Coloni brought these beliefs and presuppositions with him into his investigation. His conclusions in mining Mark 13 for the *ipsissima verba* of Jesus are therefore not unexpected. He saw Mark 13:5-31 as consisting of Jewish-Christian apocalyptic teachings that did not come from the historical Jesus and were in fact contrary to his teachings. Since then numerous scholars have followed Coloni and found behind Mark 13 a Jewish or Jewish-Christian source consisting of something like 13:7-8, 12, 14-22, 24-27; or 13:5b-8, 12-16, 19-22, 24-27; or 13:6, 7b, 8, 12, 13b-20a, 22, 24-27; or 13:7-8, 14-20, 24-27.[41]

Although some scholars continue to argue that a Jewish apocalyptic source lies behind Mark 13, the great majority of scholars today believe that the material in this chapter has a Christian origin. Those who see a Jewish-Christian source behind the Little Apocalypse find this primarily in 13:7-8, 14-20 and 24-27.[42] The trend, however, is to acknowledge that much or most of this material had its origin in the teachings of Jesus. There is nothing in the material describing the judgment of Jerusalem that is not already found in earlier prophetic predictions and descriptions of such an event (cf. Ps 74:3-7; 137:1-9; Jer 7:14; 9:11; 26:6, 17-19; 32:24-29; 52:4-30; Ezek 4:1-3; Mic 3:9-12). There is also nothing in this material that must be attributed to a post–A.D. 70 reading of descriptions of the actual event back on the lips of Jesus. On the contrary, there are several things missing in Jesus' prediction that indicate Mark 13 was written before A.D. 70. One is the lack of any mention of the large part that fire played in the destruction of the temple and the city.[43] Another is the omission of any mention of the violent, intramural fighting among various Jewish groups during the siege. Still another is the lack of any mention of the thousands of Jews that were crucified by the Romans outside the city walls. Finally, the reference to praying that the destruction not take place during the winter (13:18) would be most strange if written after A.D. 70, since the destruction of the city took place in the summer of that year.[44]

---

[41]For an attempt to reconstruct the presynoptic eschatological tradition of Jesus' teachings, see David Wenham, *The Rediscovery of Jesus' Eschatological Discourse*, Gospel Perspectives 4 (Sheffield: JSOT Press, 1984).

[42]See Robert H. Stein, *Mark*, BECNT (Grand Rapids: Baker Academic, 2008), p. 583n4.

[43]Compare *J.W.* 6.249-87.

[44]Grayston, "Mark XIII," p. 377, also points out that "the situation presented by the four temporal clauses [13:7, 11, 14, 18] . . . in no way corresponds to the situation after A.D. 70, indeed they set the scene of a dramatic episode before the Jewish revolt at a time when the likely outlines of a conflict could be discerned though the actual clash had not yet developed."

The main purpose of the mining of Mark 13 for its sources was in order to discover material earlier than the Gospel of Mark. Having come to the conclusion that Mark was the earliest Gospel, and therefore by implication that it contained the more primitive form of the Jesus traditions, it was hoped that further literary criticism would lead to even more primitive forms of the tradition. This material would then bring us even closer to the *ipsissima verba* and *vox* of Jesus. Thus "investigating Mark 13 for information about its sources" is in reality the basic tool for "investigating Mark 13 for information about the historical Jesus."

It must be acknowledged that behind much of the investigation for the sources of Mark 13 lay the desire to separate the teachings of Jesus from the eschatological material found there. This was especially true during the heyday of theological liberalism in the nineteenth century. There was also, however, in the search for the primitive sources of Mark 13 a genuine desire by many to arrive at the *ipsissima verba* and *vox* of Jesus. The degree of success achieved in this effort is much debated, and unfortunately the results were often predicated not on the research itself but on the presuppositions brought to the research.

Other goals in the search of the sources of Mark 13 can be simply literary in nature. Source critics are interested not only in what written sources may underlie our present Mark but also in discovering any oral sources that may underlie the Gospel. Literary critics can investigate Mark 13 to observe its metaphorical terminology. When is the language to be interpreted literally? When does it use nonliteral, hyperbolic terminology? Where do we find poetry? Are the two questions in 13:4 to be understood as examples of synonymous parallelism? Step parallelism? How does the argument of Mark 13 proceed? Should we define the language as apocalyptic in nature or prophetic? Does it matter how we define it?

It is evident that the investigation of Mark 13 can be done for various reasons and with different purposes in mind, but in the investigation of Mark 13 is there "a still more excellent way"?

Seeking the Meaning of the Evangelist in Writing Mark 13

Whereas research in the Gospels in the late eighteenth, nineteenth and early twentieth centuries focused on ascertaining the actual teachings of Jesus (the pursuit of his *ipsissima verba* and *vox*) and the sources of the present Gospels (what in the past has been called "literary criticism"), in the 1930s "we . . . come to a period when scholars have become more interested in the teaching of our Gospels than in their analysis, and this is reflected in their treatment of Mark 13."[45] With the advent of redaction criticism in the 1950s and 1960s scholarly research began to focus on the unique role of the final authors in the composition of our present Gospels. Whereas the quest for the historical Jesus concentrated its attention on the first setting of the Gospel tradition—that is, the life and teachings of Jesus of Nazareth—and the investigation of the oral and written sources underlying our present Gospels focused on the second setting of the Gospel tradition—that is, what it could learn about the early church—redaction criticism focused its attention on the third and final setting of the Gospel traditions.[46] Unlike the quest for the historical Jesus and form criticism, which either ignored the work of the Evangelists in the writing of the Gospels or deleted it because it was a distraction to the investigation, redaction criticism concentrated its attention and interest on the work of the Evangelists and their contribution to the Gospel traditions. It sought the unique theological emphases and purposes of Matthew, Mark and Luke in writing their Gospels and the setting in life in which they were written. It was the diversity of the Synoptic Gospels that now became the center of attention. Not surprisingly, their unity and their lookalike character, which caused earlier scholars to refer to them as the "Synoptic Gospels" and place them side by side in the New Testament, were minimized. With respect to Mark, redaction critics concentrated on the Evangelist's unique contribution to the present Gospel rather than his main emphases, which more often than not coincided with those of Matthew and Luke.

In seeking to understand the meaning of the present text of Mark 13, there is much debate as to where this meaning is to be found. There are advocates for each of the three components of the communicative act being the determiner of the meaning of Mark 13. Between the 1930s and 1960s a movement arose called the "New Criticism" which argued that meaning is the property of the text. Readers therefore began to focus their attention on under-

---

[45]Beasley-Murray, *Jesus and the Last Days*, p. 142.
[46]The original German expression used to designate such a setting in life is *Sitz im Leben*.

standing the present form of the text itself. What the original author sought to communicate by the text was irrelevant. Texts were seen as autonomous works and were to be treated as isolated works of literary art. The biggest problem with the claim that meaning is a property of the text is the question of how an inanimate object (primarily papyrus/parchment and ink) can "mean" anything. Meaning is the result of reasoning and thought. Thus, whereas a written text can convey a meaning, it cannot will a meaning because, as an inanimate object, it cannot think! Only the other two components of communication (the author and reader) can reason and think. Thus a willed meaning is only possible from the two human components of the communicative process.

During the latter part of the twentieth century, a reader-response hermeneutic became popular in literary circles. This view argued that it is the reader who determines the meaning of a text. Until the reader bestows meaning on a text, a text is essentially dead or in hibernation. It is the reader who actualizes a text and gives it a meaning. As a result a text has not a single meaning, but as many meanings as readers choose to give it. Readers are encouraged to bring their own causes and interests to texts, for in so doing they give life and passion to texts. Consequently, we come across readings of texts that are Marxist, feminist, egalitarian, gay, lesbian, liberationist, postcolonial, ecological, social-scientific and so on, though the authors of those texts had no such concerns in mind when they wrote and may have actually opposed such views.[47]

The present work is based on a traditional, author-oriented hermeneutic and seeks to understand the meaning that the author of Mark 13 sought to convey to his first-century readers.[48] It is not primarily an attempt to investigate its subject matter as to what the historical Jesus taught concerning the destruction of the temple and Jerusalem or the coming of the Son of Man. It is not an attempt to learn about the history of the early church between the resurrection of Jesus and the time when Mark was written. At times these

---

[47]For a more detailed discussion of these three alternative views as to where the meaning of a text is to be found, see Robert H. Stein, *A Basic Guide to Interpreting the Bible: Playing by the Rules*, 2nd ed. (Grand Rapids: Baker Academic, 2011), pp. 5-18.

[48]The present writer is in full agreement with Hengel, "Tasks," p. 83, who states, "The definitive starting point [for the study of a text] remains, despite 'reader response,' the early Christian author, that is, what he meant and intended in view of his addressees, hearers, and readers."

issues may be discussed briefly but only if they help us better understand the Markan meaning of the text that we possess. The goal of this work is to understand what the author of the Gospel we call Mark meant and sought to convey by the present text of Mark 13. The issue of who actually wrote the second Gospel in the New Testament is not important for our quest of the meaning of Mark 13. The meaning of this chapter is what its author, whoever he may have been, meant by the Greek text he has given to us. Concerns about authorship usually involve the significance or value a person places on the message of the author. If the Mark of Acts, in whose home the early church met (Acts 12:12), wrote this Gospel, its value as an accurate and reliable account of the life and teachings of Jesus is considerably enhanced. If it was written by some unknown Mark whose relationship to the eyewitness reports of the Gospel witnesses is uncertain, its historical value is considerably diminished. The meaning of Mark 13, however, is not affected! The meaning of Mark 13 still means what its author meant when he wrote it, whoever the author may have been. Support for the traditional Markan authorship of the second Gospel is strong and convincing.[49] Nevertheless, in using the name "Mark" in this work, we will be simply using this traditional name associated with this Gospel without making any claim as to its actual authorship.

A helpful aid in understanding the meaning of Mark 13 is to know the audience for whom Mark wrote this chapter. Information for this comes from two sources: external information (tradition) and internal information (what we can learn about the audience from the Gospel of Mark itself). The latter is the most objective, and we learn from it that:

1. The native tongue of the readers was Greek, the language of our text, and they did not know Aramaic, for Aramaic terms and expressions in the text are translated for the readers into Greek (see 3:17-22; 5:41; 7:11, 34; 9:43; 10:46; 14:36; 15:22, 34).

2. The readers were Christians. Titles such as Christ, Son of God, Son of Man, Son of David and Lord are not explained; John the Baptist comes on the scene without explanation of who he is (1:4-8); and so on.

3. The readers belonged to a church that two sons (Alexander and Rufus) of an eyewitness (Simon of Cyrene) attended (15:21).

---

[49]For a discussion of the authorship of Mark, see Stein, *Mark*, pp. 1-9.

4. The readers were familiar with places named in the Gospel (Capernaum, Tyre, Sidon, Jerusalem, Bethsaida, Caesarea Philippi, Jericho, Bethany, Bethphage, Jordan River, Judea, Galilee, the Decapolis, Gennesaret and Mount of Olives are referred to without explanation).

5. The readers were familiar with Old Testament characters (Abraham, Isaac, Jacob, Moses, Elijah, David) and the Old Testament (12:10-11, 26; 14:49).

6. The readers knew of certain leaders involved in the life of Jesus (Herod, Pilate).

7. The readers were familiar with Old Testament rituals and rites (Sabbath, Passover, Feast of Unleavened Bread, cleansing rites for a healed leper) but were ignorant of certain rituals associated with the Pharisees (7:3-4).

8. The readers were primarily Gentiles in contrast to Jews (7:3).[50]

The way the above are referred to in Mark without explanation assumes that the readers were familiar with much of this. In summary, we learn from the Gospel itself that the audience for whom the Gospel was written was Greek speaking, Gentile, Christian, and well acquainted with the Christian traditions and the Old Testament.[51]

As to the location of the Gospel's audience, this is less certain. Ancient tradition for the most part states that the Gospel was written in Rome for the Roman church. (The much-debated *Secret Gospel of Mark* and John Chrysostom argue that Mark was written in Alexandria.) Certain internal evidence suggests Rome as the likely place of origin. This includes the presence of certain "Latinisms": mat (2:4, 9, 11; 6:55), basket (4:21), legion (5:9, 15), soldier of the guard (6:27), denarius (6:37; 12:15; 14:5), fist (7:3), pitcher (7:4), tax (12:14), penny (12:42), centurion (15:39, 44, 45), to satisfy (15:15), scourge (15:15), praetorium (15:16). The "frequency [of these words] in Mark suggests that the Evangelist wrote in a Roman environment."[52] The mention of the "fourth watch" (6:48 ESV; 13:35) involves a Roman reckoning of time and sug-

---

[50]For a more detailed discussion of the audience of Mark, see Stein, *Mark*, pp. 9-12.
[51]Morna D. Hooker, "Trial and Tribulation in Mark XIII," *BJRL* 65 (1982): 98, argues that the readers of Mark were probably "Christians who are unduly excited and agitated by eschatological expectation." For a discussion of the difficulty in trying to obtain a more detailed picture of the "Markan community," see Michael F. Bird, "The Markan Community, Myth or Maze? Bauckham's *The Gospel for All Christians* Revisited," *JTS* 57 (2006): 474-86.
[52]Vincent Taylor, *The Gospel According to St. Mark* (London: Macmillan, 1952), p. 45.

gests a Roman environment since the Jewish reckoning of time involves only three watches of the night. The other main alternative for the audience of Mark involves the church in Syria. In the present work, neither of the two most suggested audiences will be assumed. Certain conclusions found in the concluding summary of the previous paragraph may at times be referred to, but the question of the exact location of the audience will be left open.

2

Key Issues Involved in Interpreting Mark 13

As is evident from the start, Mark 13 is not a self-standing, isolated flyleaf or fragment. Whatever its origin, in its present form it is preceded by twelve chapters and followed by three more. There is a sense in which it possesses a certain completeness in itself: it has an introduction (13:1-2) and a conclusion (13:37), and the following material has a new introduction (14:1). It possesses a unity in its content in that it involves two issues: the destruction of the temple (and the city of Jerusalem) and the coming of the Son of Man. It is also, however, connected to what precedes and serves as the conclusion to 11:1–13:37. As a result of the failure of Israel and above all its leadership to fulfill its calling and bear fruit (11:12-25; 12:1-12, 38-40), and because of its hostility to God's anointed (11:1-19, 27-33; 12:13-17, 18-27; cf. 14:1-2, 10-11), there will result judgment (13:1-23, 28-31) and the coming and vindication of the Son of Man (13:24-27, 32-37). These two themes will be repeated in the following chapters (14:8-9, 23-25, 27-28, 62; 15:39; 16:1-6 and 14:58; 15:29, 38).

The genre of this chapter is much debated. Is it an apocalyptic work, comparable to Daniel 7–12, *1 Enoch* 37–71 and 2 Esdras 13? While there are similarities between Mark 13 and such works, certain elements characteristic of apocalypses are lacking, including a heavenly vision, a review of human history divided into predetermined segments, the presence of angelic intermediaries, heavenly battles, reference to the nation of Israel being delivered from its enemies, the resurrection of the dead, judgments involving punishment and rewards, bizarre imagery, and pseudonymity. There is furthermore no clear distinction between the genre of prophecy and that of apocalyptic. This is evident in that the book of Revelation, which is rightly referred to as an "apocalypse" (*apokalypsis,* Rev 1:1), more often calls itself a "prophecy" (*prophēteias,* Rev 1:3; 22:7, 10, 18-19; cf. 22:6). Little is gained by seeking to classify Mark 13 as an apocalypse or a prophecy, for the same rules apply to interpreting the cosmic, exaggerated and metaphorical language found in both.[1] Attempts to classify Mark 13 as a testament or farewell discourse[2] are unconvincing because the chapter lacks such characteristics of these two genres as reflection on past events, summoning of disciples and reference to the speaker's impending death or departure. A better description for Mark 13 is to define it, along with the rest of Mark, as an example of "historical narrative."[3] Ultimately, however, "the label we put on this chapter matters little."[4]

Most scholars agree that Mark 13 deals with the Evangelist's understanding of Jesus' teachings concerning the destruction of the temple and the coming of the Son of Man. The basic issue involves which passages deal with the former and which deal with the latter. Some of the main suggestions for understanding this chapter are in the following outlines.

Outline 1

13:5-23: The destruction the temple (and Jerusalem)

13:24-27: The coming of the Son of Man

13:28-31: A parable concerning the destruction of the temple (and Jerusalem)

13:32-37: A parable concerning the coming of the Son of Man[5]

---

[1] See David E. Aune, *Apocalypticism, Prophecy, and Magic in Early Christianity: Collected Essays* (Grand Rapids: Baker Academic, 2008), pp. 1-12, for a helpful discussion. Note especially this statement: "Toward the end of the last century it became increasingly evident that prophecy and apocalyptic exhibit both continuity and discontinuity" (p. 6).

[2] See Francis J. Moloney, *Glory Not Dishonor: Reading John 13-21* (Minneapolis: Fortress, 1998), pp. 4-7; Joel Marcus, *Mark 8-16. A New Translation with Introduction and Commentary,* AYB (New Haven: Yale University Press, 2009), p. 867; C. Clifton Black, *Mark,* ANTC (Nashville: Abingdon, 2011), p. 264.

[3] Adela Y. Collins, *The Beginning of the Gospel: Probings of Mark in Context* (Minneapolis: Fortress, 1992), pp. 1-38 (esp. pp. 23-28).

[4] Morna D. Hooker, *The Gospel According to Saint Mark,* BNTC (Peabody, MA: Hendrickson, 1991), p. 299.

[5] William L. Lane, *The Gospel According to Mark,* NICNT (Grand Rapids: Eerdmans, 1974), pp. 455-84; Larry W. Hurtado, *Mark,* NIBC (Peabody, MA: Hendrickson, 1983), pp. 212, 222-25; Ben Witherington III, *The Gospel of Mark: A Socio-Rhetorical Commentary* (Grand Rapids: Eerdmans, 2001), pp. 340, 348-50, who refers to an ABA'B' pattern.

Outline 2

13:5-13: The destruction of the temple (and Jerusalem)

13:14-27: Tribulation preceding the coming of the Son of Man and his coming

13:28-31: A parable concerning the destruction of the temple (and Jerusalem)

13:32-37: A parable concerning the coming of the Son of Man[6]

Outline 3

13:5-23: The destruction of the temple (and Jerusalem)

13:24-27: The coming of the Son of Man

13:28-37: Parables concerning the coming of the Son of Man[7]

Outline 4

13:5-23: Events preceding the coming of the Son of Man

13:24-37: The coming of the Son of Man[8]

Outline 5

13:1-37: The destruction of the temple (and Jerusalem) and the establishment of a new order (without a literal coming of the Son of Man)[9]

---

[6]James R. Edwards, *The Gospel According to Mark*, PNTC (Grand Rapids: Eerdmans, 2002), pp. 385-86, who also refers to an ABA'B' pattern. Compare also Walter W. Wessel and Mark L. Strauss, *Mark*, rev. ed., EBC (Grand Rapids: Zondervan, 2010), p. 916.

[7]George R. Beasley-Murray, *Jesus and the Last Days: The Interpretation of the Olivet Discourse* (Peabody, MA: Hendrickson, 1993), pp. 364-65; Rudolf Pesch, *Das Markusevangelium, Part 2: Kommentur zu 8,27–16,20*, 2nd ed., HTKNT (Freiburg: Herder, 1981); Hooker, *Mark*, pp. 320-24; Francis J. Moloney, *The Gospel of Mark: A Commentary* (Peabody, MA: Hendrickson, 2002), p. 251-53, 272; Adela Y. Collins, *Mark: A Commentary*, Hermeneia (Minneapolis: Fortress, 2007), pp. 591-619.

[8]Vincent Taylor, *The Gospel According to St. Mark* (London: MacMillan, 1952), pp. 498-524; William Hendricksen, *The Gospel of Mark*, NTC (Grand Rapids: Baker, 1975), p. 510; D. E. Nineham, *Saint Mark*, PGC (Baltimore: Penguin, 1963), pp. 343-62; James A. Brooks, *Mark*, NAC (Nashville: Broadman, 1991), pp. 204-18; Robert H. Gundry, *Mark: A Commentary on His Apology for the Cross* (Grand Rapids: Eerdmans, 1993), pp. 733-35; Craig A. Evans, *Mark 8:27–16:20*, WBC (Nashville: Nelson, 2001), p. 292; John R. Donahue and Daniel J. Harrington, *The Gospel of Mark*, SP (Collegeville, MN: Liturgical Press, 2002), p. 378; Marcus, *Mark 8–16*, p. 867; Camille Focant, *The Gospel According to Mark: A Commentary*, trans. L. R. Keylock (Eugene, OR: Pickwick, 2012), pp. 523, 529, 542-56.

[9]Ezra Palmer Gould, *A Critical and Exegetical Commentary on the Gospel According to St. Mark*, ICC (New York: T & T Clark, 1896), pp. 240-41; Thomas R. Hatina, "The Focus of Mark 13:24-27: The Parousia or the Destruction of the Temple?" *BBR* 6 (1996): 43-66; N. T. Wright, *Jesus and the Victory of God* (Minneapolis: Fortress, 1997), pp. 339-68; Scot McKnight, *A New Vision for Israel: The Teachings of Jesus in National Context* (Grand Rapids: Eerdmans, 1999), pp. 120-55; and Thomas R. Hatina, *In Search of a Context: The Function of Scripture in Mark's Narrative*,

Outline 6

13:1-31: The destruction of the temple (and Jerusalem) and the establishment of a new order

13:32-37: Unknown time of the coming of the Son of Man and the end[10]

The varied interpretations of Mark 13 found in commentaries, books and articles that deal with this passage are due to a number of reasons. One involves the difference in the goals that the interpreters have. The goal of this work is not to excavate Mark 13 for various subject matters, whether historical or literary. The goal is rather to understand what the author of Mark sought to teach his readers by the Jesus traditions that he chose to include in this chapter, his arrangement of these traditions and his editorial work in the recording of this material. Thus there will be obvious differences between the goal of the present work and those that seek to reconstruct the actual words of Jesus and understand what he meant by those words. This is true whether such a reconstruction is radical or conservative. This will also be true with respect to those whose goal is to dissect Mark 13 literarily into various pre-Markan sources.

Yet even among scholars who have the same goal understanding the meaning of the author of Mark 13, there exist many differences about how this chapter should be interpreted. This is due in part to the presence of numerous *crux interpreta* in the chapter. The most important of these involves the two questions found in 13:4. Does Mark understand "When will [these things] be?" (13:4a) and "What will be the sign that all these things are about to be accomplished?" (13:4b) as a two-part question in which the same issue (the destruction of the temple) is addressed? This would then be a tautology and essentially an example of synonymous parallelism. Or does he understand them as two different questions in which the second introduces something quite different (the coming of the Son of Man) not found in the first (the destruction of the temple). This would then be an example

---

JSNTSS 232 (Sheffield: Sheffield Academic Press, 2002), p. 348, who summarizes this view: "The entire discussion (vv. 5-37) [should] be viewed as a response by the Markan Jesus to the disciples' two-part question in v. 4 . . . [i.e.] as referring to the destruction of the Temple."

[10]R. T. France, *Jesus and the Old Testament: His Application of the Old Testament Passages to Himself and His Mission* (Downers Grove, IL: InterVarsity Press, 1971), pp. 231-33; and R. T. France, *The Gospel of Mark*, NIGTC (Grand Rapids: Eerdmans, 2002), pp. 500-46.

of step parallelism.[11] And how do these two questions relate to 13:2-3 and Jesus' statement concerning the destruction of the temple (and by implication the destruction of Jerusalem)? Is the antecedent of "these things" and "all these things" (13:4) Jesus' statement about the temple's destruction in 13:2 ("Do you see these great buildings? Not one stone will be left here upon another; all will be thrown down")? Also, how do the two questions in 13:4 relate to 13:5-37? Should we understand them as unrelated, as Victor of Antioch suggested—that is, that the disciples in 13:4 asked one question but Jesus in 13:5-37 answered another?[12] Or does Mark understand 13:5-37 as Jesus' answer to 13:4? If the latter is true, we should not be too quick to assume that Mark 13:30 ("Truly I tell you, this generation will not pass away until all these things have taken place") is an error. Finally, what does Mark understand in 13:5-37 as the "sign" referred to in 13:4?

With respect to 13:5-23 several important issues arise that effect one's understanding and interpretation of these verses. Does Mark intend that the temporal statements and exhortations that follow in 13:7-8 and 9, 11a and 11b, 14a and 14b-16, and 21ab and 21c-23 be understood by his readers as directed to them—that is, to the "external context" of the Gospel? Or does he intend that his readers understand them as having been given by Jesus to the "historical" disciples of 13:3 (Peter, James, John and Andrew) concerning what they will experience after his death and resurrection up to the time of the destruction of the temple—that is, to the "internal context" of the Gospel? For Mark's readers the specific advice Jesus addressed to his disciples (such as fleeing Judea in 13:14) was not relevant, but perhaps that advice contained relevant implications such as:

- Jesus, the Son of God, knew and predicted the destruction of Jerusalem
- Jesus forewarned Jewish Christians in Jerusalem and Judea to flee at the appearance of a certain sign—the abomination of desolation (13:14-16)—so that they could escape the coming destruction of the city (by fleeing to Pella?)

---

[11]This assumes that the destruction of the temple and the coming of the Son of Man, while different events, are related in that they are both end-time events inaugurated by the coming of the kingdom of God in Jesus' ministry.

[12]Victor of Antioch, *The Catena in Marcum: A Byzantine Anthology of Early Commentary on Mark*, ed. W. R. S. Lamb, TENTS 6 (Leiden: Brill, 2012), p. 399; cf. Evans, *Mark 8:27–16:20*, p. 303.

- Jesus promised Jewish believers in Judea that he would give the Holy Spirit to them and he would also do the same for Mark's readers in their times of persecution and trial (13:11)
- Jesus foretold that suffering awaited his disciples and followers in Judea, and that suffering awaited all his followers, so that Mark's readers should prepare themselves for similar trials and tribulation (cf. 13:7-12 and 8:34-38)

In the interpretation of Mark 13 it must be remembered that this chapter is a mixture of three different settings in life: the first involving the teaching of the historical Jesus to his disciples, the second involving the situation of the early church between the death and resurrection of Jesus and the writing of the Gospels, and the third involving the situation in which and for which the Evangelist Mark wrote his Gospel. The Evangelist was not a radical creator of the Jesus traditions contained in his Gospel. He did not create them *de novo*, out of nothing. He was not writing a work of fiction. He was rather writing a work that is best defined as historical narrative. Thus he was not master of his material in the same sense that writers of fiction are masters of theirs. On the contrary, he was limited by the teachings of the historical Jesus of Nazareth in the first setting in life and by the Jesus traditions being transmitted in the second, which both he and his readers knew well. The fact that two sons of an eyewitness (Mk 15:21) were present among his readers placed further restraints on his freedom as a writer. Finally, it should be noted that Mark considered the Jesus traditions he was reporting as sacred traditions: "Heaven and earth will pass away, but [Jesus'] words will not pass away" (13:31).

For the present writer, Mark is best understood as a conservative editor of the Jesus traditions. Interpreters will be spared numerous misunderstandings of the material in Mark if they keep in mind that the material found in Mark 13:14-23 was directed by Jesus to Jewish Christians, who, when the time came and they saw the sign of the abomination of desolation taking place, should flee Jerusalem and Judea to avoid its coming destruction with its attendant suffering and horror. A mirror reading of this material, which understands Mark 13:14-23 as being addressed by Mark directly to his readers rather than as an account of Jesus' words addressed to his original audience, ignores the fact that the exhortations in these verses would make no sense for Mark's readers. They were Gentile Christians who did not live in Judea.[13] Thus, whereas an exhortation to flee the coming destruction of the temple and Jerusalem in 13:14 would make good sense to Jesus' original audience, it would not have direct relevance for Mark's readers.

Other more specific exegetical issues encountered in 13:5-23 are: What do "come in my name" (13:6) and "endures to the end" (13:13) mean? What does the "abomination of desolation" refer to? Is the appearance of the abomination of desolation in 13:14 the "sign" referred to in 13:4? Should the expression "has not been from the beginning of the creation that God created until now, no, and never will be" (13:19) be interpreted literally? Is this expression used elsewhere in the Bible? If so, is it used here as exaggerated language to emphasize the horror of the coming "holocaust" of A.D. 70?

As to 13:24-27, should this language be understood literally or symbolically? Is such cosmic language found elsewhere in the Bible? If so, how is it used? Is the coming of the Son of Man in these verses referred to elsewhere in the Bible? Was the coming of the Son of Man from heaven a familiar teaching to Christians at the time Mark was written? If so, how would Mark's readers have been inclined to interpret this passage? How should the temporal sequence in 13:24, "But in those days, after that suffering," be understood? Is "in those days" a technical term?

In 13:28-31 does Mark understand the fig tree blossoming as indicating the time of Jerusalem's destruction or the Son of Man's coming? Should "these things" in 13:29a and "all these things" in 13:30 be interpreted in light of the use of these same two expressions in 13:4? And how should Jesus' emphatic statement "Truly . . . this generation will not pass away until all these things have taken place" be interpreted?

For 13:32-37, does Jesus, as the Son, truly mean that he did not know the day that the Son of Man would return? What are the theological implications of this? Finally, did Mark intend that his readers should interpret Jesus' exhortations to Peter, James, John and Andrew in 13:33-37 to "watch" as directed toward them, the readers?

---

[13]See the discussion of the audience of Mark on pp. 39-41 above.

In the coming chapters we will deal with these and other questions in our attempt to understand the Markan meaning of 13:1-37. We will attempt to complete the following sentence: "I, Mark (the author), have written Mark 13:1-37, because . . ." We will do so using the following outline:

13:1-4: Jesus' prediction of the destruction of the temple (and Jerusalem)

13:5-23: The coming destruction of the temple (and Jerusalem) and the sign preceding it

13:24-27: The coming of the Son of Man

13:28-31: The parable of the fig tree and the coming destruction of the temple (and Jerusalem)

13:32-37: The parable of the watchman and the exhortation to be alert for the coming of the Son of Man

3

Jesus' Prediction of the Destruction of the Temple (and Jerusalem)

Mark 13:1-4

TEXT AND INTRODUCTION

¹As he came out of the temple, one of his disciples said to him, "Look, Teacher, what large stones and what large buildings!" ²Then Jesus asked him, "Do you see these great buildings?¹ Not one stone will be left here upon another; all will be thrown down." ³When he was sitting on the Mount of Olives opposite the temple, Peter, James, John, and Andrew asked him privately, ⁴"Tell us, when will [these things]² be, and what will be the sign that all these things are about to be accomplished?"

In chapters 11–12 of his Gospel, Mark describes Jesus' actions and teachings in Jerusalem and the temple. Whereas the Gospel of John refers to several visits by Jesus to Jerusalem during his ministry (2:13-4:45; 5:1-47; 7:1-10:40; 12:12-20:31), Mark refers to only one (11:1-16:8). This is due to the overall arrangement of his Gospel into three geographical units: Jesus' ministry in Galilee (1:1-8:21),³ his journey to Jerusalem (8:22-10:52) and his

---

¹It is best to interpret this sentence as a rhetorical question rather than a rebuke, "Are you marveling at these great buildings?" contra Robert H. Gundry, *Mark: A Commentary on His Apology for the Cross* (Grand Rapids: Eerdmans, 1993), pp. 735-36; and R. T. France, *The Gospel of Mark*, NIGTC (Grand Rapids: Eerdmans, 2002), p. 496.

²The NRSV translates *tauta* as "this," but it is better translated "these things" to parallel the way *tauta* is translated later in the sentence, where *tauta* . . . *panta* is rendered "all these things." In 13:29-30 the NRSV correctly translates *tauta* and *tauta panta* "these things" and "all these things."

³It is best to see 8:22 as beginning a new section. This allows the three subsections of 1:14-8:21 (1:14-3:6; 3:7-6:6a; 6:6b-8:21) to begin with a summary (1:14-15; 3:7-12; 6:6b), followed by a call or sending out of the disciples (1:16-20; 3:13-19; 6:7-13), and to end with a reference to the unbelief Jesus encountered (3:6; 6:1-6a; 8:14-21).

ministry in Jerusalem (11:1-16:8). Consequently, the Jesus traditions that had geographical designations associated with Galilee[4] are placed by Mark in 1:1–8:21, and those involving geographical places in Jesus' journey to Jerusalem[5] were placed in 8:22–10:52. Those that involve Jesus' ministry in Jerusalem and Judea[6] therefore had to be placed in 11:1–16:8.

The various geographical designations listed in Mark may not all have been tied to the pre-Markan Jesus traditions available to him. Some of them, especially those that betray the hand of Mark, may be due to his work as editor of these materials.[7] It is probable, however, that when adding them, Mark was doing so based on a broad knowledge of the life of Jesus rather than simply creating geographical designations out of the air. The geographical knowledge of Galilee and Judea found in the Gospel is quite good, and arguments against its accuracy usually are due to a lack of awareness of Mark's methodology.[8] It

---

[4]Sea of Galilee (1:16; 2:13; 3:7; 4:1, 35; 5:1, 21; 6:32-34; 7:31; 8:10); Capernaum (1:21; 2:1); Gerasa (5:1, the exact reading of the Greek text here is uncertain); Nazareth (6:1); King Herod, the ruler of Galilee (6:14); Bethsaida (6:45); Gennesaret (6:53); Tyre and Sidon (7:24, 31); the Decapolis (7:31); Dalmanutha (8:10, the exact reading of the Greek text here is uncertain).

[5]Caesarea Philippi (8:27); passing through Galilee (9:30); Capernaum (9:33); Judea (10:1); the eastern side of the Jordan River (10:1); the road going up to Jerusalem (10:32); Jericho (10:46). Cf. also Bethsaida (8:22), which is mentioned as the point of departure.

[6]Jerusalem (11:1, 11, 15, 27); Bethphage (11:1); Bethany (11:1, 11-12; 14:3); the Mount of Olives (11:1; 13:3); the temple (11:11, 15, 27; 12:35, 41; 13:1, 3); Gethsemene (14:32); the celebration of the Passover which could only be eaten in Jerusalem (14:1, 12); Jesus' trial before the high priest and religious leaders (14:43, 53; 15:1); the praetorium or governor's headquarters (15:16); Golgotha (15:21).

[7]See especially the following summaries (1:39; 3:7-12; 6:53; 9:30-32; 10:32-34) and seams (1:14, 16, 21; 2:1, 13; 5:1, 21; 6:1; 7:24, 31; 8:22, 27; 9:33; 10:1, 46; 11:1, 12, 15, 27; 12:35; 13:1, 3; 14:1, 3, 12, 32, 53; 15:16).

[8]One of the alleged geographical errors of Mark is found in 7:31. Here Mark refers to Jesus returning from the region of Tyre "by way of Sidon towards the Sea of Galilee, in the region of the Decapolis." If one looks at a map of these areas it would be like going from Portland to Denver by way of Seattle and the Great Plains. See Joel Marcus, *Mark 1–8: A New Translation with Introduction and Commentary*, AYB (New Haven, CT: Yale University Press, 2002), p. 472. However, in describing the journey Mark first lists the place of departure (Tyre), then the goal of the journey which is indicated by "towards" (*eis*) (the Sea of Galilee) and that this was "by way of" Sidon and the Decapolis. We have the same claim that Mark erred geographically in 10:1 where we read, "He left that place [Capernaum, 9:33] and went to the region of Judea and beyond the Jordan." Once again we should note that Mark first lists the point of departure ("that place"), then the goal of the journey "to" (*eis*) (the region of Judea), by way of the eastern side of the Jordan River. (This was a frequent route used by Jews traveling from Galilee to Judea or the reverse in order to avoid going through Samaria.) A final example is found in 11:1 where Jesus and the disciples "were approaching [*eis*] Jerusalem, at Bethphage and Bethany, near the Mount of Olives." If one again observes that Mark mentions Jerusalem first because it is the ultimate goal of their journey, not because it is the first place they will come to, the alleged error disappears. For further discussion, see Robert H. Stein, *Mark*, BECNT (Grand Rapids: Baker Academic, 2008), pp. 357-59, 454, 503.

is obvious that Mark was limited in the placement of some of his material due to his geographical scheme. Other constraints that he faced were chronological (the trial, death and resurrection had to come at the end) and the desire to place similar materials together (1:21-45 healing stories; 2:1–3:6 controversy stories; 4:1-34 parables; 4:35–5:43 Jesus' lordship over nature, demons, disease and death). Whether all the controversy stories in 11:27-33 and 12:13-37[9] occurred together and in that order and whether all the teachings in 13:5-37 occurred together or whether they came to Mark as a unit is uncertain. Fortunately, these issues are of minor importance in our quest to understand the meaning of the present text of Mark 13.

In the Jerusalem accounts in chapters 11–12 Mark portrays a dark picture of the hostility and unbelief encountered by Jesus. Like the prophets before him, Jesus experiences the hostility of the religious leaders.[10] The material in these two chapters reveals Israel's and especially her religious leaders' failure to fulfill their calling to bear fruit for God. This is evident in Jesus' "cleansing" of the temple (11:15-19), which had been made a "den of robbers" by the chief priests and scribes (11:17-18). Mark wants his readers to understand that the action of Jesus in overturning the tables of the money changers and those selling pigeons for sacrifice was not primarily an act of purification and reformation but one of judgment. He does this by dividing the story of the cursing of the fig tree into two parts (11:12-14 and 11:20-25) and placing the overturning of the tables of the merchants by Jesus (11:15-19) in between. This "Markan sandwich" indicates that the Evangelist wants his readers to interpret Jesus' activity in the temple as similar to his cursing of the fig tree. Seeking fruit and finding nothing but leaves, Jesus judged the tree and cursed it. Seeking fruit in the temple (cf. 11:11 and 15) and finding nothing but the dry leaves of sterile worship in which the weightier matters of justice, mercy and faith were lacking (cf. Mt 23:23-24; Mic 6:8), he judged it, and that judgment is described in 13:1-37.[11]

---

[9]It may be that 12:28-34 is better described as a pronouncement story because of Jesus' positive response to the scribe in 12:34a.

[10]Note how Matthew prepares his readers for this by placing Mt 23:29-39 before his inclusion of the material contained in Mk 13:1-37 into Mt 24:1-44.

[11]Jacob Chanikuzhy, *Jesus, the Eschatological Temple: An Exegetical Study of Jn 2,13-22 in the Light of the Pre-70 C.E. Eschatological Temple Hopes and the Synoptic Temple Action*, CBET (Leuven: Peeters, 2012), p. 183, rightly points out that "the evangelists link the temple action with the death of Jesus [and this] shows that Jesus' action in the temple was highly offensive and serious

In 12:1-12, the only major parable in Mark found outside chapter 4, we find the same message of judgment. The various similarities between this parable and the parable of the vineyard in Isaiah 5:1-7[12] would have caused the audiences of both Jesus and Mark to see allegorical significance in some of its details. The vineyard would be understood as representing Israel ("for the vineyard of the LORD of hosts is the house of Israel," Is 5:7) and its privileged position of being God's chosen people. The owner of the vineyard is "the LORD of hosts" (Is 5:7). Mark's readers would also find allegorical significance in the following details of 12:1-12: the tenants are the leaders of Israel; the servants who are shamed, abused, beaten and killed are the prophets; the son is Jesus, the Son of God; the killing of the son is the crucifixion of Jesus; the destruction of the tenants represents the coming destruction of the temple and Jerusalem; and the vineyard being given to others represents the establishment of a new people of God consisting of a remnant of believing Israel and Christian Gentiles.[13] This parable of the vineyard in Mark portrays a similar understanding as that found in Jesus' cleansing of the temple in 11:11-19. An owner seeks fruit from the tenants of his vineyard, but instead of receiving his deserved fruit his messengers are shamed, beaten and killed. As a result he will come and bring judgment on the tenants, and the vineyard will be given to others (12:9). This parable also prepares Mark's readers for the destruction of the temple and Jerusalem that Jesus foretells in chapter 13. The response Jesus receives to his parable (12:12)

---

enough to seal his fate. Neither a messianic claim nor a prophetic call for repentance would have immediately brought about the death of Jesus and this suggests that the temple action of Jesus was a symbolic enactment of the eschatological destruction of the temple."

[12]The three most popular Old Testament books among the Jews of Jesus' day were Deuteronomy, the Psalms and Isaiah, which happen to be the three Old Testament books most quoted in the New Testament.

[13]Several scholars argue against the view that Israel is portrayed in the parable as being replaced by Gentiles as the people of God. See Craig A. Evans, *Mark 8:27–16:20*, WBC (Nashville: Nelson, 2001), p. 237, and France, *Mark*, p. 462n17, who argue that the tenants of the parable represent the leadership of Israel and not the Jewish people in general. Matthew, one of the earliest known interpreters of this parable, however, understands the new tenants as being Gentiles, for he adds at the end of the parable, "Therefore I tell you, the kingdom of God will be taken away from you and given to a people that produces the fruits of the kingdom" (Mt 21:43). Much of the debate on this issue appears to involve the difference between what Jesus may have meant by this parable and what the later Evangelists understood and taught concerning it. We must keep in mind that we are discussing what Mark meant to convey by this parable to his mostly Gentile readers. He may very well have interpreted the parable in light of such teachings as found in Acts 13:44-47; Rom 9:11-16; 10:19; 1 Pet 2:9-10; cf. Mt 22:8-10.

from the chief priests, scribes and elders (11:27, the antecedent of "them" in 12:1) is similar to what is found elsewhere in Mark. The religious leaders seek to kill him (cf. 3:6; 14:1), but the people hear him gladly (12:37) and are the major impediment to the religious leaders carrying out their plan (12:12; cf. 11:18; 14:1-2). In these two chapters preceding Mark 13, the Evangelist reveals the reason for the divine judgment coming on the temple and Jerusalem. As he writes his Gospel, that judgment is already now coming to fruition.

The present section of Mark 13 consists of a change of scene (13:1a), an exclamation by one of the disciples concerning the magnificence of the temple (13:1b), a prophecy of Jesus concerning the destruction of the temple (13:2), and after another transitional verse (13:3), a twofold question by the disciples for clarification of the prophecy as to when this would take place and what the sign preceding its fulfillment would be (13:4).

MARK 13:1: JESUS LEAVES THE TEMPLE, AND THE DISCIPLES REMARK ABOUT THE TEMPLE'S MAGNIFICENCE

The opening verse of this chapter marks a geographical change of scene from the temple to the Mount of Olives (13:3). Mark ties 13:1-37 to the completed ministry of Jesus in the temple described in chapters 11–12 by a genitive absolute, "As he came out of the temple."[14] Since Jesus is the main character in the Gospel, Mark focuses his attention on him, not the disciples (12:43), for this Gospel is about "Jesus Christ, the Son of God" (1:1).[15] Such a journey would probably have involved leaving the temple and Jerusalem through the Golden Gate in the eastern wall of Jerusalem, down the Kidron Valley and up the Mount of Olives. Mark has no interest, however, in describing the path of this journey, except to state that Jesus now leaves temple, thus ending his mission there (11:1–12:44), and proceeds to the Mount of Olives. There is no hint in Mark that this leaving the temple is to be interpreted symbolically as an act in which Jesus gives the temple over to judgment. Various

---

[14]Other genitive absolutes appearing in Markan introductory seams are found in 1:32; 4:35; 5:2, 21; 6:2, 54; 8:1; 9:9; 10:17, 46; 11:12, 27; 14:3 (2x), 17, 22, 43; 15:33; 16:1.

[15]Cf. how in Mark 5:2–6:1a the disciples, who are with Jesus (5:1; 6:1b), are mentioned only in 5:31, 37, 40, and that the focus is entirely on Jesus: "he," "him," "his"—5:2, 8, 9 (2x), 10 (2x), 12, 13, 17, 18 (3x), 19 (2x), 21(2x), 22 (2x), 23, 24 (3x), 27, 28, 30 (4x), 31, 32, 33 (2x), 34, 35, 36, 37 (2x), 38, 39, 40 (3x), 41 (2x), 43 (2x); 6:1 (2x); "Jesus" (5:6, 7, 15, 20, 21, 27, 30, 36); "Son of the Most High God" (5:7); "Lord" (5:19, cf. 5:20); "you," "your" (5:23 [2x], 31 [2x]); "teacher" (5:35); "I" (5:41); "my," "me" (5:30, 31).

actions and teachings of Jesus in chapters 11–12 teach this, especially the cleansing of the temple and its interpretation by the cursing of the fig tree (11:12-25) and the parable of the wicked tenants (12:1-12). It is not, however, the statement of Jesus leaving the temple in 13:1 but Jesus' teachings in 13:2, 5-23 and 28-31 that teach that the temple and Jerusalem were judged and awaited divine destruction. Jesus left the temple on several occasions in 11:11, 19. If Mark wanted to give theological significance to Jesus leaving the temple in 13:1, he could have written "As he left the temple *for the last time*" or added something like Matthew 23:37-39/Luke 13:31-35.

As Jesus was leaving the temple, Mark reports an exclamation of one of the disciples concerning its magnificence, "Look, Teacher, what large stones and what large buildings!" The exclamation is not to be likened to a tourist's awestruck expression at seeing this magnificent sight, a wonder of its day, for the first time. The disciples would have seen this every day since their entry into Jerusalem as they traveled back and forth from Jerusalem to Bethany (11:1, 12, 19, 20, 27). Furthermore, as observant Jews, they would have celebrated numerous Passovers in Jerusalem. Such an exclamation would have been quite normal, no matter how often one saw the temple. Some of the stones used in building the western wall and extending the courtyard westward were extraordinary, to say the least. Josephus refers to some stones in the temple complex as being 45 x 5 x 6 cubits (67 x 7 x 9 feet) and others as 25 x 8 x 12 cubits (37 x 12 x 18 feet) in size.[16] In the 1990s an archeological exploration of the temple foundations revealed a large stone bolstering the second tier of the western foundation wall that was 42 x 14 x 11 feet in size and estimated to weigh 600 tons.[17] Two other stones were found that were 40 and 25 feet long. The magnificence and beauty of the Herodian temple was known throughout the world and made some of the seven wonders of the world pale in comparison.[18]

---

[16] See *J.W.* 5.224; *Ant.* 15.392.

[17] Dan Bahat, "Jerusalem Down Under: Tunneling Along Herod's Temple Mount Wall," *BAR* 21, no. 6 (1995): 30-47.

[18] Cf. *b. Sukkah* 51b: "Our Rabbis taught . . . he who has not seen Jerusalem in her splendour, has never seen a desirable city in his life. He who has not seen the Temple in its full construction has never seen a glorious building in his life." Cf. also Josephus, *Ant.* 15.396; *J.W.* 5.222-23. Tacitus in *Fragments of the Histories* 2 describes the temple as "a mighty temple . . . a consecrated shrine, which was famous beyond all other works of men." On the issue of the authenticity of this fragment and others, however, T. D. Barnes, "The Fragments of Tacitus' *Histories*," *Classical*

Mark 13:2: Jesus Predicts the Temple's Destruction

The massive stones used in building the temple and the temple mount gave a sense of permanence and impregnability to it. Thus Jesus' response would have seemed not just surprising but incredible. Although only the destruction of the temple is spoken of and no mention is made concerning the destruction of Jerusalem, the destruction of the city must be assumed as accompanying the destruction of the temple. No enemy would be allowed by the Jews living in Judea and Jerusalem to destroy the most sacred building of Judaism. They would defend the temple to the death, and before an enemy could reach it, they would have to destroy the mighty fortress of Jerusalem and overcome its massive walls and towers and its dedicated citizenry. Old Testament prophecies frequently tie the destruction of Jerusalem and the temple together.

> Therefore because of you
> Zion shall be plowed as a field;
> Jerusalem shall become a heap of ruins,
> and the mountain of the house a wooded height. (Mic 3:12; cf. Jer 26:17-18)

> The Lord has scorned his altar,
> disowned his sanctuary;
> he has delivered into the hands of the enemy
> the walls of her palaces . . .
> The LORD determined to lay in ruins
> the wall of daughter Zion . . .
> he caused rampart and wall to lament;
> they languish together.
> Her gates have sunk into the ground;
> he has ruined and broken her bars. (Lam 2:7-9; cf. also Jer 7:13-20)[19]

The authenticity of Jesus' prophecy in 13:2 is supported by other prophecies of Jesus concerning the destruction of the temple in Mark and the other Gospels. It is raised at his trial: "We heard him say, 'I will destroy this temple

---

Philology 72 (1977): 224-31, raises serious questions and urges caution as to their use. Nevertheless, George R. Beasley-Murray, *Jesus and the Last Days: The Interpretation of the Olivet Discourse* (Peabody, MA: Hendrickson, 1993), p. 383, points out that "the temple complex in Jerusalem was probably the most awesome building in the ancient world."

[19]Cf. also 2 Kings 25:9; 2 Chron 36:19; Jer 26:6, 9; Dan 9:26; 11:31; 2 Macc 14:33; Tob 14:4; *1 Enoch* 90:28.

that is made with hands, and in three days I will build another, not made with hands'" (Mk 14:58), and as a jeer from the crowd at his crucifixion: "Aha! You who would destroy the temple and build it in three days" (Mk 15:29). We also find in John 2:19 in response to a request for a sign from Jesus' opponents that "Jesus answered them, 'Destroy this temple, and in three days I will raise it up.'" Even outside the Gospels we find a reference to this saying of Jesus by the elders and scribes in their accusation against Stephen, "We have heard him [Stephen] say that this Jesus of Nazareth will destroy this place and will change the customs that Moses handed on to us" (Acts 6:14). Other prophecies of Jesus predicting the destruction of Jerusalem and the temple are found in Matthew 23:38/Luke 13:35: "See, your house is left to you, desolate" and in Luke 19:43-44: "Indeed, the days will come upon you, when your enemies will set up ramparts around you and surround you, and hem you in on every side. They will crush to the ground, you and your children within you, and they will not leave within you one stone upon another; because you did recognize the time of your visitation from God." From these prophetic pronouncements and Jesus' symbolic act of "cleansing" the temple, it is clear that Mark's recording of Jesus' prediction in 13:2 concerning the destruction of the temple and Jerusalem was not a *de novo* creation but based on " a stream of tradition which attributed to Jesus apocalyptic predictions against the temple and the city."[20]

The presence of other prophecies in the time of Jesus that predicted the coming destruction of the temple and Jerusalem lends further credence to Jesus also having done so. One of the most famous is that of a Jesus, the son of Ananias, who shortly before the war with Rome predicted the coming destruction. Josephus tells us that

> four years before the war . . . one Jesus, son of Ananias . . . standing in the Temple, suddenly began to cry out,
>
> A voice from the east,
> a voice from the west,
> a voice from the four winds,
> a voice against Jerusalem and the sanctuary,
> a voice against the bridegroom and the bride,
> a voice against the people! (*J.W.* 6.301; cf. also 306, 309)

---

[20]John R. Donahue, *Are You the Christ? The Trial Narrative in the Gospel of Mark*, SBLDS 10 (Missoula, MT: Society of Biblical Literature, 1973), p. 108.

The presence of numerous other predictions in the intertestamental literature, Josephus and the rabbinic literature[21] indicates that Jesus' predictions of the destruction of Jerusalem and its temple are no more prophecies after the fact than are these others.

Jesus' prediction in 13:2 is not understood by Mark as a simple, unfortunate consequence of the Roman pursuit of complete control of the Middle East. It is not merely the result of a foolish attempt for Jewish independence from Roman rule and its predictable outcome. On the contrary, Mark writes as a theologian and tells of the divine and ultimate cause for this catastrophe. Even as the destruction of Jerusalem and the temple in 587 B.C. involved both an immediate and an ultimate cause, so did their destruction in A.D. 70. In 587 B.C. the immediate cause was Babylon and Nebuchadnezzar; in A.D. 70 it was Rome and Titus. In both instances the ultimate cause was the same. God was judging the nation for its sin. "Mark's setting of the prophecy at this point inevitably confirms the impression that the ruin of the temple is the divinely ordained judgment upon Israel for its rejection of the word of God brought by Jesus."[22] There is also a sense in which Mark understands this prediction of Jesus not merely as declarative in nature but causative as well. Jesus not only predicts the destruction of Jerusalem and the temple; he brings it about! This is clearly seen in 14:58 ("We have heard him say, '*I* [italics added to indicate the emphatic nature of the first person pronoun in Greek] will destroy this temple that is made with hands'"), and 15:29 ("Aha! You who would destroy the temple").

The reference in Jesus' prophecy to there not being one stone remaining on another has been interpreted literally by some. This has caused difficulty, since any visitor to Jerusalem can still see some of the foundation stones that made up the western and the eastern walls of the city still lying one on the other. Consequently, they have interpreted 13:2 as referring only to the temple sanctuary itself. Such an interpretation, however, ignores the use of

---

[21] For a listing of these predictions and their content, see Evans, *Mark 8:27–16:20*, pp. 296-97. For a more detailed discussion, see Craig A. Evans, "Predictions of the Destruction of the Herodian Temple in the Pseudepigrapha, Qumran Scrolls, and Related Texts," *Journal for the Study of the Pseudepigrapha* 10 (1992): 89-147.

[22] Beasley-Murray, *Jesus and the Last Days*, pp. 353-54; cf. Larry W. Hurtado, *Mark*, NIBC (Peabody, MA: Hendrickson, 1983), p. 213.

exaggeration and hyperbole in prophecy, especially judgment prophecies.[23] In 2 Samuel 17:13 we find a similar description of "total" destruction in which "not even a pebble [of the destroyed city] is to be found there." The LXX translation refers to not even a stone being left, and in the LXX translation of Haggai 2:15 the exact same Greek expression "a stone upon a stone" is found and involves the rebuilding of the temple. All this suggests that the language in Mark refers to the "total" destruction of the temple and the city by the Romans. Josephus describes the systematic destruction of the temple and the city decreed by Titus:

> Caesar ordered the whole city and the temple to be razed to the ground, leaving only the loftiest of the towers ... and the portion of the wall enclosing the city on the west ... to indicate to posterity the nature of the city and of the strong defenses which had yet yielded to the Roman prowess. All the rest of the wall encompassing the city was so completely leveled to the ground as to leave future visitors to the spot no ground for believing that it had ever been inhabited.[24]

The result was such that any Jew in A.D. 71 looking from the Mount of Olives at the city of Jerusalem and the ruined temple would have agreed that Jesus' prediction in 13:2 had indeed been fulfilled.

Mark 13:3-4: The Disciples' Two-Part Question—The Key for Understanding Mark 13

Although some scholars choose to connect these verses with what follows,[25] they are best understood as associated with 13:1-2 and completing the introduction to the teachings of Jesus that follow in 13:5-37. Although within 13:1-4 the hand of Mark is seen most clearly in the seams of 13:1a and 13:3a, the entire passage for the most part betrays the style and vocabulary of the Evangelist. Nevertheless, the exclamation in 13:1c, the prophecy in 13:2 and something like the two questions in 13:4

---

[23]See Robert H. Stein, *A Basic Guide to Interpreting the Bible: Playing by the Rules*, 2nd ed. (Grand Rapids: Baker Academic, 2011), pp. 138-47.
[24]Josephus, *J.W.* 7.1-4; see also *J.W.* 6.352-55, 363-64, 409-13.
[25]See Evans, *Mark 8:27-16:20*, pp. 300-314, and James R. Edwards, *The Gospel According to Mark*, PNTC (Grand Rapids: Eerdmans, 2002), pp. 389-95, who deal with 13:3-13 together; and France, *Mark*, pp. 497-546, and Adela Y. Collins, *Mark: A Commentary*, Hermeneia (Minneapolis: Fortress, 2007), pp. 594, 602, who deal with 13:3-37 together.

are probably traditional. Fortunately, our task in trying to understand this passage is not dependent on reconstructing the history of how it came into existence—that is, its *Traditionsgeschichte*—but in correctly interpreting the present text that we possess.

Mark 13:3 serves as a transitional verse presupposing 13:1-2 and linking these two verses with the two questions of 13:4. Together these four verses serve as the introduction to 13:5-37 and are the interpretative key for understanding the teachings of Jesus that follow. The reference to "Peter, James, John, and Andrew" is unusual in two ways. For one, the usual group that forms Jesus' inner circle in Mark is "Peter, James, and John" (5:37; 9:2; 14:33). The two sets of brothers are mentioned together in 1:16-18 and 19-20 (cf. also 3:16-20 where they are listed as the first four of the twelve disciples and occur in the same order as we find in 13:3). The mention of Andrew here and the unusual order may betray the traditional nature of this verse. The reference to Jesus teaching the disciples "privately" (*kat' idian*) recalls 4:34; 6:31, 32; 7:33; 9:2, 28, which all bear a heavy Markan imprint.[26]

The location of Jesus' teachings in Mark 13 is the Mount of Olives. The reference to this site and Jesus sitting and teaching in full view of the temple and the city with their "large stones and . . . large buildings" (13:1) adds to the drama of what the disciples are about to ask (13:4) concerning Jesus' prophecy of the temple's destruction (13:2) and his answer to their questions (13:5-37). Since on their arrival in Jerusalem Jesus and the disciples had traveled daily from Bethany to the temple and passed over the Mount of Olives (11:11-12), the scene has every reason to be authentic. Although references to the Mount of Olives are found in several Old Testament passages (Ezek 11:22-25; Zech 14:4-5; cf. also *Ant.* 20.169-72; *T. Naph.* 5.1), Mark makes no reference or allusion to them, so that the mention of this site serves primarily as an opportunity for him to focus attention on the temple and city whose destruction Jesus has just foretold. Jesus' sitting indicates that he is assuming the posture of a teacher (3:32; 4:1; 12:41; Mt 5:1; 26:55; Lk 4:20-21; 5:3; cf. also Jn 8:2).

---

[26]For other instances in Mark where Jesus taught the disciples and worked miracles away from the crowds, see 1:29-31; 4:10, 35-41; 5:40-43; 6:7-13, 30-32, 33-37, 45-52; 7:24-30; 8:14-21, 27-33; 9:2-13, 30-32, 33-37, 38-41, 42-50; 10:10-11, 17-31, 32-45; 11:12-14, 20-25; 12:41-44; 14:3-9, 12-42; cf. also 1:40-45.

With Mark 13:4 we come to the single most important verse in this chapter. It is the key for interpreting what follows,[27] for Mark wants his readers to understand that the teachings of Jesus in 13:5-37, and especially in 13:5-23, are his answer to the disciples' two-part question[28] in this verse. The two parts form a parallelism and refer back to 13:2:

when will these things [*tauta*] be? (author's translation)

what will be the sign that all these things [*tauta . . . panta*] are about to be accomplished?[29]

The two questions are both natural and legitimate.[30] Despite Mark 8:11-12, in which Jesus rejects the desire of the Pharisees for him to justify his claims and teachings by performing a miraculous sign, there is no criticism by Jesus in the present account with respect to the disciples' request for a sign.[31] Their *request* for a sign stands in sharp contrast with the *demand* of the Pharisees for Jesus to do a sign! Furthermore, a sign is referred to in Mark 13:14 and 28-29 concerning when all these things are about to take place. Rather than rebuking the disciples for their two questions, Jesus proceeds to answer their request in 13:5-37. In 13:14 he reveals the sign (the abomination of desolation) and the time ("when you see") when these things will take place. The reason that Jesus accepts the disciples' request for a sign is because this is not an attempt to test him or to satisfy their curiosity and supply additional eschatological information to complete their apocalyptic time charts. It is rather in order to be forewarned and prepared for the ful-

---

[27]Cf. Rudolf Pesch, *Naherwartungen: Tradition und Redaktion in Mk 13*, KBANT (Düsseldorf: Patmos, 1968), p. 101, who states that the disciples' question in 13:4 is the *wichtige Schlüssel zum Verständnis der eschatologischen Rede*—that is, "the important key for the understanding of [Jesus'] eschatological discourse [in Mark 13]."

[28]So Adela Y. Collins, *The Beginning of the Gospel: Probings of Mark in Context* (Minneapolis: Fortress, 1992), p. 77.

[29]Francis J. Moloney, *The Gospel of Mark: A Commentary* (Peabody, MA: Hendrickson, 2002), p. 253, refers to three questions of 13:4 concerning the destruction of the temple and Jerusalem, the time of the end of the world and the sign preceding the end. It is best, however, to refer to this material as two questions according to their grammatical form, rather than three according to their content.

[30]For the legitimacy of a request for a sign in certain instances, cf. Ex 3:12; 7:8-13; 2 Kings 19:29; Is 7:11-17; 2 *Baruch* 25:1-4; 2 Esd 4:52.

[31]Thus there is no justification for Timothy J. Geddert saying that the request for a sign in 13:4 is "an expression of the disciples' misguided expectation." *Watchwords: Mark 13 in Markan Eschatology*, JSNTSS 26 (Sheffield: Sheffield Academic Press, 1989), p. 57.

fillment of Jesus' prophecy in 13:2. The disciples' twofold question does not seek information as to "how" this destruction will take place. The Old Testament provided more than enough information in its many descriptions of how this took place when Jerusalem was destroyed in 587 B.C. and the tribulations preceding and following this event.[32]

The exact relationship between the expressions "these things" and "all these things" is much debated. Do they have the same referent? If so, what are they referring to? Or does "all these things" have a different referent? Unless one assumes that Jesus' answer is unrelated to the disciples' question—that is, that the disciples asked one question and Jesus answered another[33]—the first question must have as its referent "these things" just mentioned in 13:2, that is, the destruction of the temple. As to "all these things" in the second question, what relationship, if any, does it have with the "these things" in the immediately preceding question? Does "all these things" have a different referent than "these things"? Does it refer to something different than the destruction of the temple or to something in addition to that destruction? Could Mark in the second question be referring not only to the destruction of the temple (13:2) but also to the coming of the Son of Man and the end of all things (13:24-27)?

"Recognition of the dual nature of Jesus' answer will go a long way toward solving the difficulties of the discourse and arriving at a sound interpretation. His answer applied first to events in the near future, especially the destruction of Jerusalem and its temple in A.D. 70, second to the end of the world and his own return."[34]

---

[32]Cf. 2 Chron 36:15-21; Neh 2:11-17; Jer 4:16-31; 9:19-22; 12:7-13; 15:1-9; 21:1-10; 25:11-14; 27:1-22; 39:1-10; 52:1-30; Lam 1–2; Ezek 4–5; Zech 14:2.

[33]So Evans, *Mark 8:27–16:20*, p. 303. Perhaps the earliest one to suggest this was Victor of Antioch. See *The Catena in Marcum: A Byzantine Anthology of Early Commentary on Mark*, ed. W. R. S. Lamb, TENTS 6 (Leiden: Brill, 2012), p. 399, on Mark 13:4.

[34]So James A. Brooks, *Mark*, NAC (Nashville: Broadman, 1991), p. 208. Compare also Johann Albrecht Bengel, *Gnomon of the New Testament* (New York: Sheldon, 1862), 1:362 on Mark 13:4; Werner H. Kelber, *The Kingdom in Mark: A New Place and a New Time* (Philadelphia: Fortress, 1974), pp. 111-13; William Hendricksen, *The Gospel of Mark*, NTC (Grand Rapids: Baker, 1975), p. 514; Rudolf Pesch, *Das Markusevangelium, Part 2: Kommentur zu 8,27–16,20*, 2nd ed., HTKNT (Freiburg: Herder, 1981), p. 275; Josef Ernst, *Das Evangelium nach Markus*, RNT (Regensburg: Pustet, 1981), p. 370-71; Morna D. Hooker, *The Gospel According to Saint Mark*, BNTC (Peabody, MA: Hendrickson, 1991), pp. 305-6; Beasley-Murray, *Jesus and the Last Days*, pp. 386-89; John Painter, *Mark's Gospel: Worlds in Conflict*, NTR (London: Routledge, 1997), pp. 170-71; Adela Y. Collins, "The Apocalyptic Rhetoric of Mark 13 in Historical Context,"

In the above interpretation do we have an example of step parallelism in which the second line possesses a broader, more comprehensive meaning and advances the first line a step higher? Or, on the other hand, could "these things" and "all these things" be synonymous expressions and both refer to the destruction of the temple predicted by Jesus in 13:2? In the latter instance we would have essentially an example of synonymous parallelism.[35]

In favor of understanding "all these things" as referring to something more than the destruction of the temple is the close association of the coming of the Son of Man in 13:24-27 with the events described in 13:5-23. There are also warnings to watch for the coming of the Son of Man in 13:32-37. As we will see in our later discussion of these verses, the event described in 13:24-27 is both separated ("after that [tribulation]") and connected with ("but in those days") the destruction of the temple in 13:5-23. In addition, certain descriptions of the destruction coming on Jerusalem in 13:5-23 seem to describe more than what took place in A.D. 70: the gospel must first be proclaimed to all nations (13:10), the abomination of desolation must first take place (13:14), a "great" tribulation must come such as never was nor will be again (13:19) and false messiahs must appear (13:22). These passages will be discussed in the exegesis of 13:5-23 where the attempt will be made to demonstrate that they are all part of Mark's portrayal of the events surrounding the destruction of Jerusalem in A.D. 70.

There are several arguments in favor of interpreting the two questions in 13:4 as having the same referent in mind. The only difference is that the first asks *when* this event will take place (13:4a) and the second asks concerning

---

Biblical Research, 41:13; Collins, *Mark*, p. 602; M. Eugene Boring, *Mark*, NTL (Louisville: Westminster John Knox, 2006), pp. 354-55; Edward Adams, *The Stars Will Fall from Heaven: Cosmic Catastrophe in the New Testament and Its World*, LNTS 347 (New York: T & T Clark, 2007), pp. 140-41; Joel Marcus, *Mark 8–16: A New Translation with Introduction and Commentary*, AYB (New Haven, CT: Yale University Press, 2009), pp. 873-74; Walter W. Wessel and Mark L. Strauss, *Mark*, rev. ed., EBC (Grand Rapids: Zondervan, 2010), pp. 916, 919; Camille Focant, *The Gospel According to Mark: A Commentary*, trans. L. R. Keylock (Eugene, OR: Pickwick, 2012), p. 526; cf. also W. D. Davies and Dale C. Allison, *A Critical and Exegetical Commentary on the Gospel According to Saint Matthew*, ICC (New York: T & T Clark, 1991), 3:331.

[35]So Lloyd Gaston, *No Stone on Another: Studies in the Significance of the Fall of Jerusalem in the Synoptic Gospels* (Leiden: Brill, 1970), p. 12; William L. Lane, *The Gospel According to Mark*, NICNT (Grand Rapids: Eerdmans, 1974), pp. 447-55; R. T. France, *Jesus and the Old Testament: His Application of the Old Testament Passages to Himself and His Mission* (Downers Grove, IL: InterVarsity Press, 1971), p. 231; France, *Mark*, pp. 506-7; John R. Donahue and Daniel J. Harrington, *The Gospel of Mark*, SP (Collegeville, MN: Liturgical Press, 2002), p. 368.

the *sign* preceding this event (13:4b). The referent, however, is the same. It is the destruction of the temple (and Jerusalem) referred to in 13:2. Some of the arguments in favor of this interpretation are:

(1) The expression "all these things" (13:4b) is associated with a sign, and the only clear "sign" referred to in 3:5-37 is the appearance of the abomination of desolation in 13:14. The question, "What will be the sign that all these things are about to be accomplished?" is answered in 13:14 by "when you *see*." Signs are something one "sees," and the first thing Mark points out as being seen after 13:4 is the abomination of desolation,[36] and this signals believers to flee Judea immediately in order to escape the destruction Jesus has predicted in 13:2.

(2) Certain advice given in 13:5-23 is totally inapplicable with respect to the coming of the Son of Man in 13:24-27, as traditionally understood. How will fleeing from Judea to the mountains (13:14-16), being pregnant or nursing a child (13:17), or the particular time of the year (13:18) have any bearing whatsoever with the events associated with the parousia? In the final judgment will pregnant women be worse off than those who are not pregnant? Will God judge people more severely in winter than in summer? Will being in the mountains be better than being in a city? The answer to these questions is "No!" But if we interpret these instructions as given by Jesus to Jewish believers in Judea and Jerusalem concerning the events of A.D. 70,[37] they make perfectly good sense, for they tell Jesus' original hearers how they should respond to the appearance of the abomination of desolation that will precede the coming destruction of the temple and Jerusalem. If one interprets the coming of the Son of Man as a metaphorical description of this destruction, the problem is resolved, but, as will be argued below, such an interpretation is not convincing.[38]

(3) The expressions "these things" (*tauta*) and "all these things" (*tauta . . . panta*) in 13:4 are used again in 13:29 ("these things" [*tauta*]) and 30 ("all these things" [*tauta panta*]). It is unlikely that this is accidental, and it is best to

---

[36]The references to "watching" in 13:5, 9, 33 ("beware") and 23 ("be alert") use a different verb (*blepō*) and possess a totally different meaning. They are imperatives referring to heeding Jesus' teachings in this chapter, not a reference to seeing something with one's eyes. They are furthermore an appeal to one's will, not one's eyesight. Attempts to see the coming of the Son of Man in 13:24-27 as the sign referred to in 13:4b lose sight of the fact that the phenomena described in these verses are not precedents or preliminary events pointing to this event but accompaniments of the event itself. See Lane, *Mark*, p. 448; Beasley-Murray, *Jesus and the Last Days*, p. 307.

[37]Note that the audience of 13:3-4 (the four disciples, us) is the audience Jesus addresses in 13:5 (them).

[38]See pp. 113-18.

interpret them as synonyms. The second reference to "these things" in 13:29 involves an injunction by Jesus to take note that "when you see [*hotan idēte*] these things taking place, you know that he/it is near, at the very gates." This recalls the earlier injunction in 13:14 to note "when you see" (*hotan idēte*) associated with the revealing of the "sign," referred to in 13:4b—the coming of the abomination of desolation in 13:14. The interchangeableness of "these things" and "all these things" is witnessed to by the fact that, whereas the "sign"—that is, "when you see"—is associated with "these things" in 13:29, in 13:4b it is associated with "all these things."

> Mark 13:4b—"what will be the sign that *all these things* are?" (italics added)

> Mark 13:29—"when you see *these things* taking place" (italics added)

Furthermore, whereas "all these things" in 13:30 deals with the "when" and supplies the answer ("this generation will not pass away"), in 13:4a the "when" is associated with "these things."

> Mark 13:4a—"*when* will *these things* be?" (author's translation)

> Mark 13:30—"*this generation will not pass away* until *all these things* have taken place" (italics added)

The interchangeability of these two expressions in 13:4b ("all these things") and 13:29 ("these things") and the interchangeability of the two expressions in 13:4a ("these things") and 13:30 ("all these things") argues strongly that Mark understands them as being synonymous expressions and having the same referent—the destruction of the temple (and Jerusalem).

(4) Another important piece of evidence in the pursuit of the meaning of "these things" and "all these things" is found in the earliest known commentary of Mark 13:4, the Gospel of Luke. If, as the majority of scholars maintain, Luke used the Gospel of Mark as one of his sources in writing his Gospel (cf. Lk 1:1-4), his understanding of Mark 13:4 is most helpful. Side by side the two parallels sections read as follows:

> Mark 13:2—"Do you see *these* [*tautas*] great buildings? Not one stone will be left here upon another; all will be thrown down." (italics added)

> Luke 21:6—"As for *these things* [*tauta*] that you see . . . not one stone will be left upon another; all will be thrown down." (italics added)

Mark 13:4a—"Tell us, when will *these things* be?" (author's translation)

Luke 21:7b—"Teacher, when will *these things* be?" (author's translation)

Mark 13:4b—"and what will be the sign that *all these things* [*tauta panta*] are about to be accomplished?" (italics added)

Luke 21:7c—"and what will be the sign that *these things* [*tauta*] are about to take place?" (author's translation)

It is clear that Luke understands "these things" in 21:6 as referring to the temple and the structures associated with it, for the only available antecedent of the expression is the "temple" and its "beautiful stones" and "gifts" referred to in 21:5. The following reference to "these things" (*tauta*) in 21:7b must be interpreted as referring to "these things" (*tauta*) in 21:6 and thus also to the destruction of the temple. His third mention of "these things" (*tauta*; "this" in NRSV) in 21:7c has as its antecedent "these things" (*tauta*; "this" in NRSV) in 21:7b and must therefore be interpreted as having the same referent: the destruction of the temple (and Jerusalem). Since the third "these things" in Luke 21:7c has as its parallel "all these things" in Mark 13:4b, this indicates that Luke understood Mark's "these things" and "all these things" as being synonymous.

(5) In contrast to Luke, Matthew appears to understand Mark's "all these things" in 13:4b as including something more than the "these things" of 13:4a.[39] The two parallel passages are:

Mark 13:4a—"Tell us, when will *these things* be?" (author's translation)

Matthew 24:3b—"Tell us, when will *these things* be?" (author's translation)

Mark 13:4b—"and what will be the sign that *all these things* are about to be accomplished?" (italics added)

---

[39]C. E. B. Cranfield, *The Gospel According to Mark*, CGTC (New York: Cambridge University Press, 1959), p. 394, argues that Matthew understands Mark correctly here. But for the present writer, it is Luke, not Matthew, who understands Mark correctly here! Matthew has enlarged the focus of the second question to include additional material concerning the coming of the Son of Man (Mt 24:37–25:46) that he adds to Mark 13:1-37. Contrast Luke who in copying the second part of the disciple's question indicates that he understands it as synonymous with the first part by using "these things" (*tauta*) again. He understands Mark's "all these things" (*tauta panta*) in the second part of the disciples' question as the same as "these things" (*tauta*) in the first part, and this involves the destruction of the temple (Mk 13:1-2; Lk 21:5-6).

Matthew 24:3c—"and what will be the sign *of your coming and of the end of the age?*" (italics added)

It appears from Matthew's modification of Mark 13:4b that he wanted the second part of the question in Mark 13:4b to serve as an introduction for the additional parousia material that he included in his version of the Olivet Discourse. It is clear that Matthew has added to Mark 13 a considerable amount of material dealing with the coming of the Son of Man not found in Mark or Luke.[40] This fits well the organizational pattern he used in writing his Gospel. That pattern involves an alternation between narrative material (chapters 1–4, 8–9, 11–12, 14–17, 19–22 [23], 26–28) and sayings or discourse material (chapters 5–7, 10, 13, 18, [23] 24–25). This is made clear by the fact that all five discourses end with a summary conclusion: "Now when Jesus had finished saying these things" (Mt 7:28-29); "Now when Jesus had finished instructing" (Mt 11:1); "Jesus told the crowds all these things in parables" (Mt 13:34-35); "When Jesus had finished saying these things" (Mt 19:1); "When Jesus had finished saying all these things" (Mt 26:1). Matthew's addition of supplementary material on the second coming contained in Matthew 24:37–25:46 to the material he found in Mark 13:1-37 (Mt 24:1-36) probably caused him to enlarge the boundaries of the two-part question of the disciples in 13:4 and add a specific reference to the coming of the Son of Man and the end of the age. Whether he thought that Mark's "all these things" did not refer to the coming of the Son of Man (so that he added "your coming and of the end of the age" in 24:3c) or whether he thought it did in fact refer to both the destruction of the temple and the parousia but wanted to make this more explicit is impossible to say.

(6) The *inclusio* found in 13:5 ("Then Jesus began to say to them") and 13:23 ("I have already told you everything") indicates that Jesus' answer to the disciples' two-part question in 13:4 ends at 13:23. The material in Mark 13:24-27 concerning the coming of the Son of Man lies outside the twofold question in 13:4 and its answer in 13:5-23. Thus the reference to the coming of the Son of Man introduces a new theme that takes place "after that [tribulation]" (13:24).

---

[40]Except for Matthew 24:45-51, which has a parallel in Luke 12:42-46, and Matthew 25:14-30, which has a parallel in Luke 19:12-27, the material in Matthew 24:37–25:46 dealing with the coming of the Son of Man is unique to his Gospel. Note also that the two parallel passages in Luke appear in entirely different locations in his Gospel than the parallel passages do in Matthew.

(7) A relevant passage often overlooked in the discussion but that sheds light on Mark's grammatical style is found in Mark 11:28. Here we find two consecutive questions that are related in terminology and refer to the same issue using synonymous parallelism. Jesus is asked, "By what *authority* are you doing *these things* [*tauta*]? Who gave you this *authority* to do *them* [*tauta*]?" Since 13:4 is a similar example of two consecutive questions using similar terminology followed by a single answer, the case can be made that it also should be interpreted as an example of synonymous parallelism.[41] Additional examples in which consecutive questions are found in Mark where the second question is essentially a repetition of the first are:

> "Then do you also fail to understand? Do you not see?" (7:18)

> "How much longer must I be among you? How much longer must I put up with you?" (9:19)

> "Are you asleep? Could you not keep awake one hour?" (14:37)

In 8:17b-18 we even find an example in which five consecutive questions are found in which the four following questions are again essentially a repetition of the first: "Do you still not perceive or understand? Are you hearts hardened? Do you have eyes, and fail to see? Do you have ears, and fail to hear? And do you not remember?"

The above examples, and especially 11:28 where we find the same vocabulary repeated in both questions, all lend support to understanding the two questions in Mark 13:4—with their respective terminology of "these things" and "all these things"—as referring to the same event: the destruction of the temple.

(8) Of the twenty-six instances in which the expression "all these things" (*tauta panta*) occurs in the New Testament, twenty-four of them have its referent occurring before the expression.[42] In one instance it may occur before and after (Lk 21:36), and the other is the passage under discussion. This suggests that we

---

[41]Beasley-Murray, *Jesus and the Last Days*, pp. 216-17, argues that Mark 11:28 serves as an example demonstrating that "these things" and "all these things" in 13:4 have two separate referents—the destruction of the temple and the end of the world. But in Mark 11:28 "these things" and "these things" have the exact same referent. They both refer to Jesus' actions in the temple in 11:1-26. Thus the example in 11:28 argues rather that the twofold question in 13:4 should be interpreted similarly as having the same referent—the destruction of the temple.

[42]See Mt 4:9; 6:32, 33; 13:34, 51, 56; 19:20; 23:36; 24:2, 8, 33, 34; Mk 7:23; 10:20; 13:30; Lk 1:65; 2:19; 12:30; 16:14; 18:21; 24:9; Jn 15:21; Acts 7:50; 1 Cor 12:11.

probably should understand "all these things" in 13:4 as referring to the "these things" preceding it and the reference to the destruction of the temple in 13:2.

(9) Finally, it should be noted that the addition of "all" (*panta*) to "these things" (*tauta*) does not require us to interpret "all these things" as "these things plus something else" or "these things and in addition the following." It is better to interpret the "all" either as intensifying "these things," so that "all these things" means something like "every one of these things just mentioned" or as simply being a synonymous expression for "these things."

Summary

The opening setting of Mark 13:1-4 contains the following: the backdrop of the Jerusalem temple (13:1); a statement by one of the disciples concerning its magnificence and size (13:2); the reply of Jesus that the temple would be totally destroyed, so that not even one stone would be left on another (13:3); and the response of the disciples involving a two-part question as to *when* this ("these things") would take place and what the warning *sign* preceding this would be (13:4). The twofold question is the key for understanding the chapter and should be understood as "concerned solely with the destruction of the Temple as predicted by Jesus in verse 2."[43] As to the "when," Mark will first deal with the "when it is not" in 13:5-7 (see esp. 13:7c: "but the end is still to come") and 8-13. As to the "sign,"[44] it should be noted that in all the parallel accounts (Mk 13:4; Mt 24:3; Lk 21:7) the expression is in the singular, "the sign" (*to sēmeion*), whereas the events in 13:5-13 are plural in number. The identification of this singular "sign" will be given along with the "when" in 13:14, "But *when* you *see* the [abomination of desolation] set up where it ought not to be." On seeing this sign that will precede the destruction of the temple (and Jerusalem), believers living in the area should immediately flee to escape the dangers and horrors (13:15-23) soon to fall on the city. Later it will be pointed out that "this generation [i.e., the generation of Jesus' disciples] will not pass away until all these things have taken place" (13:30).

---

[43]France, *Jesus and the Old Testament*, p. 231. In this respect N. T. Wright, "In Grateful Dialogue: A Response in *Jesus & the Restoration of Israel: A Critical Assessment of N. T. Wright's 'Jesus and the Victory of God,'"* ed. Carey C. Newman (Downers Grove, IL: InterVarsity Press, 1999), p. 265, is correct: "The question with which the chapter [Mark 13] opens, and for which the previous chapters have exactly prepared us, is about the fall of Jerusalem and the temple in particular."

[44]W. A. Such points out that in the Markan introduction of chapter 13 (13:1-4) the key term *sēmeion* (sign) serves as a kind of title and catchword and points to 13:14. "The *Crux Criticorum* of Mark 13:14," *Restoration Quarterly* 38 (1996): 94.

4

The Coming Destruction of the Temple (and Jerusalem) and the Sign Preceding It

Mark 13:5-23

TEXT AND INTRODUCTION

⁵Then Jesus began to say to them, "Beware that no one leads you astray. ⁶Many will come in my name and say, 'I am he!' and they will lead many astray. ⁷When you hear of wars and rumors of wars, do not be alarmed; this must take place, but the end is still to come. ⁸For nation will rise against nation, and kingdom against kingdom; there will be earthquakes in various places; there will be famines. This is but the beginning of the birth pangs.

⁹"As for yourselves, beware; for they will hand you over to councils; and you will be beaten in synagogues; and you will stand before governors and kings because of me, as a testimony to them. ¹⁰And the good news must first be proclaimed to all nations. ¹¹When they bring you to trial and hand you over, do not worry beforehand what you are to say; but say whatever is given you at that time, for it is not you who speak, but the Holy Spirit. ¹²Brother will betray brother to death, and a father his child, and children will rise against parents and have them put to death; ¹³and you will be hated by all because of my name. But the one who endures to the end will be saved.

¹⁴"But when you see the [abomination of desolation]¹ set up where it ought not to be (let the reader understand), then those in Judea must flee to the mountains; ¹⁵the one on the housetop must not go down or enter the house to take anything away; ¹⁶the one in the field must not turn back to get a coat. ¹⁷Woe to those who are pregnant and to those who are nursing infants

---

¹The NRSV uses the expression "desolating sacrilege."

in those days! ¹⁸Pray that it may not be in winter. ¹⁹For in those days there will be suffering, such as has not been from the beginning of the creation that God created until now, no, and never will be. ²⁰And if the Lord had not cut short those days, no one would be saved; but for the sake of the elect, whom he chose, he has cut short those days. ²¹And if anyone says to you at that time, 'Look! Here is the Messiah!' or 'Look! There he is!' — do not believe it. ²²False messiahs and false prophets will appear and produce signs and omens, to lead astray, if possible, the elect. ²³But be alert; I have already told you everything."

After the two-part question of the disciples in 13:4, Mark records Jesus' answer in 13:5-23. Other examples, in which a question, comment or action of the disciples elicits a teaching response from Jesus can be found in 4:10 (4:11-34); 7:17 (7:18-23); 9:28 (9:29), 38 (9:39-41); 10:13 (10:14-16), 35 (10:36-40). In those instances in which the disciples ask Jesus a question (4:10; 7:17; 9:28), Jesus specifically answers the disciples' question; and, although some scholars argue that in 13:5-23 Jesus' answer is not specifically directed at the disciples' question in 13:4,[2] Mark gives no hint that Jesus' answer is not a direct response to the disciples' two-part question.

The teachings in 13:5-23 form a unified whole. This can be seen by the repeated command to "Beware [*blepete*] that no one leads you astray" in 13:5; "beware" (*blepete*) in 13:9; and "be alert" (*blepete*) in 13:23, which is better translated "beware" to indicate that it is the same term as in 13:5 and 9. In addition the unity of this discourse is seen in the temporal clauses tying this material together:

- 13:7—"When [*hotan de*] you hear of wars and rumors of wars . . . but the end is still to come [*oupō to telos*]"
- 13:8—"This is but the beginning of the birth pangs [*archē ōdinōn tauta*]"

---

[2]Cf. Craig A. Evans, *Mark 8:27–16:20*, WBC (Nashville: Nelson, 2001), p. 303, who states, "Jesus does not directly answer their questions concerning 'when will these things be' or 'what will be the sign when will all these things are about to be accomplished.' Jesus instead warns of deception and persecution." Cf. also Larry W. Hurtado, *Mark*, NIBC (Peabody, MA: Hendrickson, 1983), p. 213; Robert H. Gundry, *Mark: A Commentary on His Apology for the Cross* (Grand Rapids: Eerdmans, 1993), p. 738; and Megan McKenna, *On Your Mark: Reading Mark in the Shadow of the Cross* (Maryknoll, NY: Orbis, 2006), p. 172, who states, "Jesus deflects the disciples' question about the timing of the destruction of the temple, and, instead, warns the disciples of corruption in their own community."

- 13:10—"And the good news must first be proclaimed [*prōton dei kēruchthēnai to euangelion*]"
- 13:11—"When [*kai hotan*] they bring you to trial"
- 13:14—"But when [*hotan de*] you see the [abomination of desolation] ... then [*tote*] those in Judea must flee"
- 13:21—"And then if [*kai tote ean*] any one says to you" (RSV)

Finally, and even more importantly, the unity of 13:5-23 is seen by the *inclusio* found in the opening verse ("Then Jesus began to say [*legein*]") and the concluding verse ("But be alert [Beware]; I have already told [*proeirēka* —a form of *prolegein*] you everything"). These two verses form bookends enclosing the material in 13:5-23, and indicate that Mark sees this material as a unified discourse containing Jesus' answer to the questions of *when* the temple would be destroyed (13:2) and what the *sign* would be (the appearance of the abomination of desolation, 13:14) that would precede this.

It should be noted that the coming of the Son of Man in 13:24-27 lies outside the material contained in the *inclusio*. This indicates that Mark does not see the coming of the Son of Man as part of Jesus' answer (13:5-23) to the disciples' twofold question (13:4) concerning the destruction of the temple. This is further indicated by Mark's introduction to 13:24-27 in 24a, "But in those days, *after* that suffering [tribulation, RSV]." It is clear from this that the parousia neither precedes the destruction of the temple nor is simultaneous with it. Rather, it comes after it! How soon after will be discussed below in chapter five.

Some scholars see in 13:5-23 a detailed chiasmus consisting of:

A The appearance of false messianic claimants (13:5-6)

B The coming of wars and natural disasters (13:7-8)

C The mission and persecution of believers (13:9-13)

B' The coming of war and the need to flee Jerusalem (13:14-20)

A' The appearance of false messianic claimants (13:21-23)[3]

---

[3]Some scholars who see this and similar forms of a chiasmus in 13:5-23 are Jan Lambrecht, *Die Redaktion der Markus-Apocalypse: Literarische Analyse und Strukturuntersuchung*, AnBib 28 (Rome: Päpstliches Bibelinstitut, 1967), p. 173; Kenneth Grayston, "The Study of Mark XIII," *BJRL* 56 (1974): 374; Gundry, *Mark*, p. 733; Francis J. Moloney, *The Gospel of Mark: A Commentary* (Peabody, MA: Hendrickson, 2002), p. 249; Dean B. Deppe, "Charting the Future or a

While there is merit in understanding 13:5-23 as a chiasmus, there are several emphases of the discourse that are not indicated in the above outline. One is the emphasis in 13:5-13 that certain things are not to be seen as the sign preceding the imminent destruction of the temple and Jerusalem. The disciples are not to be deceived into thinking that the appearance of false messianic claimants, reports and rumors of wars, earthquakes, and famines foretell the imminent destruction of Jerusalem. These are natural events that must take place in a fallen world, but the disciples should not be alarmed, for the end—that is, the temple's and Jerusalem's destruction—is not yet imminent (13:7). Nor should they interpret their present persecution as such a sign (13:9-13). Thus another outline will be followed in the discussion of this section of Mark:

Events That Are Not Signs of the Temple's Imminent Destruction (13:5-13)

    The first non-sign: The appearance of false messianic claimants (13:5-6)

    The second non-sign: The coming of wars and natural disasters (13:7-8)

    The third non-sign: The mission and persecution of believers (13:9-13)

The Sign of the Abomination of Desolation Heralding the Temple's and Jerusalem's Imminent Destruction and the Warning to Flee Judea (13:14-20)

The Warning of False Messianic Claimants Appearing Before the Temple's and Jerusalem's Destruction (13:21-23)

A serious problem is encountered in the reading of Mark 13, and for that matter in the reading of any text involving historical narrative. This involves the question of whether injunctions and warnings in the text[4] are to be understood as being directed by the author, in this case Mark, to his intended readers or as reports of injunctions and warnings that were delivered by Jesus to his disciples. In other words, are the particular injunctions and warnings found on the lips of Jesus in 13:5-23 addressed by Mark to his readers (the "external context")? Or does Mark want his readers to understand that these warning and injunctions were addressed by Jesus during his

---

Perspective of the Present? The Paraenetic Purpose of Mark 13," *CTJ* 41 (2006): 93-94. There is considerable variety, however, as to the makeup of the suggested chiasmus.

[4]We find such injunctions in 13:5, 9, 23, 33 (which use *blepete*), and 13:7, 11, 18, 21. Cf. also 13:28 (2x), 29, 33, 35 and 37 (*grēgoreite*).

ministry to his followers (the "internal context"), who when they saw the abomination of desolation appearing in the temple were to flee Jerusalem and Judea for safety in the mountains? One of the clearest examples of interpreting the injunctions in 13:5-23 as addressed by Mark to his readers is that of Marxsen.[5] He interpreted the Gospel of Mark as the Evangelist's warning to his readers to flee Judea and go to Pella in order to escape the destruction of the temple and Jerusalem. Here they were to await the imminent coming of the Son of Man.[6] This mirror reading of Mark 13 requires that his intended readers were Jewish Christians living in Judea and Jerusalem in the late sixties. From the text of Mark, however, we learn that his readers were Gentile, not Jewish, as the explanation of Jewish customs (7:2-3, 14:12, 15:42) and Aramaic terms (3:17, 22; 5:41; 7:11; 9:43; 10:46; 14:36; 15:22, 34) clearly indicate.[7] Why would Mark explain Pharisaic religious traditions and Aramaic expressions in his Greek Gospel to Jewish Christians living in Jerusalem whose mother tongue was Aramaic? This would be like the present author writing a letter in English to his relatives in Germany and explaining to them German customs and traditions and the meaning of various German terms and phrases! Marxsen's mirror reading of Mark is clearly flawed and has rightly received little support.[8]

Unlike writers of fiction, Mark and the other Evangelists were under numerous restraints as they wrote their Gospels. One such restraint was the "facts" of the life and teaching of the historical Jesus that were known by his readers.[9] Another was the shape and content of the Gospel traditions concerning Jesus that were circulating within the Christian community. By the time Mark wrote his Gospel these traditions were in a fairly fixed form and had already begun to be treated as sacred tradition.[10] Thus Mark's readers al-

---

[5]Willi Marxsen, *Mark the Evangelist: Studies on the Redaction History of the Gospel*, trans. James Boyce et al. (Nashville: Abingdon, 1969). See especially pp. 166-89.
[6]Marxsen follows Ernst Lohmeyer, *Galiläa und Jerusalem* (Göttingen: Vandenhoeck, 1936), pp. 10-25, and Robert Henry Lightfoot, *Locality and Doctrine in the Gospels* (New York: Harper, 1937), pp. 55-65, in interpreting Mark 14:28 and 16:7 as referring to the parousia not the resurrection of Jesus. See, however, Robert H. Stein, "A Short Note on Mark XIV.28 and XVI.7," *NTS* 20 (1973): 445-52.
[7]See pp. 39-41 above.
[8]For a more conservative mirror reading of Mark 13, see Martin Hengel, *Studies in the Gospel of Mark*, trans. John Bowden (Philadelphia: Fortress, 1985), pp. 7-30.
[9]Note Luke's reference to his readers' knowledge of these traditions in his Gospel (Lk 1:4).
[10]Note how Paul claims that the tradition of the Lord's Supper he "delivered" to the Corinthians (1 Cor 11:23-26 RSV) was ultimately "received from the Lord" (1 Cor 11:23a). Yet even as the

ready possessed considerable knowledge of the material contained in his Gospel when it was read to them. As they heard his Gospel read, they also realized that some of Jesus' instructions were not directed specifically to them. They might contain relevant implications, but from what we learn from this Gospel concerning Mark's readers, the instructions given about seeing the abomination of desolation standing in the temple would not have been directed to them. The readers no doubt knew of a similar abomination of desolation from the incident recorded in Daniel 9:27; 11:31; 12:11 and 1 Maccabees 1:54, 59. This event and the subsequent cleansing of the temple in 165 B.C. were celebrated yearly, usually in December, by Jews in the eight-day festival called *Hanukkah* or "The Feast of Lights" (cf. Jn 10:22-23).[11] The injunction to flee Judea and Jerusalem on seeing the abomination of desolation, however, was neither a possibility nor concern for Mark's non-Palestinian, Gentile audiences. Thus Mark does not address these instructions to his readers, and present-day readers should not apply a mirror reading to them. Rather, Mark wants his readers to interpret the material in 13:14-20 as injunctions given by the historical Jesus to Jewish followers during his ministry. These instructions concerned events that would affect them in their lifetime (13:30) and involved the coming destruction of the temple and Jerusalem (13:2, 4).

It is essential in interpreting Mark 13 that we not assume that the Evangelist wants Jesus' injunctions in this chapter to be understood as being addressed directly to the readers of his Gospel.[12] They are not Markan creations or radically modified Jesus traditions directed at them. He expects them to be understood as instructions addressed by Jesus to Peter, James, John and Andrew concerning *when* the destruction of Jerusalem and temple would take place, and the appearance of the *sign*—the abomination of desolation—warning of their imminent destruction. On seeing this sign, they

---

Jesus traditions were delivered by the apostles to the believing community (Lk 1:1-2), the reverse was also true. The community was delivered over to that sacred tradition (Rom 6:17)!

[11]George R. Beasley-Murray, *Jesus and the Last Days: The Interpretation of the Olivet Discourse* (Peabody, MA: Hendrickson, 1993), p. 367, points out that "the memory of Antiochus Epiphanes and the deliverance from his blasphemous oppression were kept fresh in the people's mind through the annual celebration of the Festival of Dedication, just as the oppression of the Egyptian Pharaoh and the deliverance at the exodus were recalled through the annual celebration of the Festival of Passover."

[12]Whether these traditions were actually spoken by the historical Jesus during his ministry or simply found in the Jesus traditions known to the readers of Mark is not important for our discussion.

were to flee immediately from Judea and Jerusalem to safety in "the mountains" (13:14). For Mark's readers the injunctions in 13:14-20 had no direct, literal significance. They might contain relevant implications for them as well as for later readers,[13] but a simplistic, mirror-reading approach to this material will lead to confusion rather than clarity.

The first part of Jesus' answer to the disciples' two-part question involves general troubles and persecutions that do not serve as indicators that the destruction of Jerusalem is at hand.[14]

Mark 13:5-13: Events That Are Not Signs of the Temple's Imminent Destruction

Mark 13:5-6—The first non-sign: The appearance of false messianic claimants. Mark begins 13:5-23 with a typically Markan "And Jesus began to say" (RSV).[15] The imperative "Beware" (*blepete*) in 13:5 is also found in 13:9, 23 (translated as "be alert" in the NRSV), 33 (cf. also 4:24; 8:15). In all these instances it has nothing to do with the sense of sight but refers rather to the need to exercise discernment as the following translations indicate: "Beware" (NRSV), "Watch out" (NIV), "See that no one" (ESV), "Don't let anyone" (NLT), "Be on your guard" (REB), "Take care" (NJB), "Take heed" (RSV) and so on. The content of this warning is that the disciples are not to be led astray by claimants coming "in [Jesus'] name" and saying "I am he!" The unfortunate result of their appearance is that they will lead many people astray with disastrous consequences.

The claim of these pretenders can be understood in several different ways. One is that they are like the Jewish exorcists in Acts 19:13-17, who used the name of Jesus as a sort of adjuration seeking to evoke magical powers unleashed by uttering the name "Jesus" (cf. Acts 8:1-24). Another is that they may be counterfeit Christian prophets claiming that Jesus sent them ("in my name").[16] Still another possible interpretation is that they are claiming to be

---

[13]Cf. Etienne Trocmé, *The Formation of the Gospel According to Mark*, trans. P. Gaughan (Philadelphia: Westminster, 1975), p. 213n3: Mark's "aim was to exhort and warn, even where his text borders on pure description."

[14]Hurtado, *Mark*, p. 214.

[15]See Robert H. Stein, *Mark*, BECNT (Grand Rapids: Baker Academic, 2008), p. 108, for a list of examples.

[16]For other warnings in the New Testament concerning false prophets and teachers seeking to lead the church astray, cf. Mt 7:22-23; Acts 19:13-16; 2 Cor 11:3; Gal 1:7; 2:4; 6:12; Phil 3:17-19; 1 Thess

Jesus himself, returned from heaven. The most likely interpretation is that these are Jewish claimants who falsely assert that they are what Jesus really is, the Messiah or Christ.[17] This interpretation receives additional support from 13:21-22 and the parallel in Matthew 24:5, "For many will come in my name, saying, 'I am the Messiah!' and they will lead many astray."

The appearance of such false messiahs, however, should not confuse them and cause them to think that their appearance indicates that the temple's destruction is at hand (the *when*) and that their appearance is the *sign* indicating this. In the first century we know of the appearance of numerous false, messianic-like claimants in Israel. At the beginning of the century there were Theudas and Judas the Galilean (Acts 5:37; *Ant.* 17.271; *J.W.* 2.56). There was also Simon of Perea (*Ant.* 17.273-77; *J.W.* 2.57-59) and Athronges of Judea (*Ant.* 17.278-84; *J.W.* 2.60-65). Shortly before A.D. 70 there was Menahem, the Son of Judas the Galilean, who is the best known (*J.W.* 2.433-48), John of Gischala (*J.W.* 2.585-89; 4.121-27) and Simon bar-Giora (*J.W.* 4.503-44; 4.556-83), along with a host of brigands.[18] Jesus' warning to his disciples to beware of false messianic claimants and prophets was necessary both in the original setting in life, and by implication as well in the time and setting of Mark and his readers, and it has unfortunately been relevant for Christians ever since. In our goal of seeking to understand the intended meaning of Mark in this passage it is important to remember that he is recording the injunctions of Jesus to his disciples concerning the coming destruction of the temple and Jerusalem (13:2, 4). The disciples were not to confuse the appearance of such messianic claimants as indicating the destruction of Jerusalem was immediately imminent.

Mark 13:7-8—The second non-sign: The coming of wars and natural disasters. The second non-sign of the temple's and Jerusalem's imminent destruction involves war and natural disasters. It is introduced in 13:7 by a "when" (*hotan*) that picks up negatively the twofold "when" asked by the

---

5:3; 2 Thess 2:2; 1 Tim 4:1; Tit 1:10; 2 Pet 2:1-3; 1 Jn 4:1-6; 2 Jn 7; Rev 2:2; cf. also *Didache* 16:4.

[17]So Morna D. Hooker, *The Gospel According to Saint Mark*, BNTC (Peabody, MA: Hendrickson, 1991), pp. 307-8; Beasley-Murray, *Jesus and the Last Days*, p. 391; Adela Y. Collins, "The Eschatological Discourse of Mark 13," in *The Four Gospels*, ed. F. van Segbroeck et al., BETL (Leuven: Leuven University Press, 1992), p. 1132.

[18]See *J.W.* 6.281-87. For additional messianic-like figures, see Evans, *Mark 8:27–16:20*, pp. 306, 425-26.

disciples in 13:4, "When [*pote*] will these things be, and what will be sign when [*hotan*] all these things are about to be accomplished?" (ESV). It warns the disciples of other events that are not the sign that Jerusalem's destruction is imminent. A second "when" (*hotan*) in 13:11 will introduce the third non-sign of Jerusalem's destruction. War and natural disaster are frequently found in prophetic descriptions of the end times. They, along with famine and disease, are part of the repertoire for prophetic predictions of the day of the Lord.[19] There is no warrant for interpreting 13:7 as referring to a specific war, such as the coming war between Jews and the Roman army that led to the destruction of Jerusalem.[20] The plural "wars" indicates that this is a general statement, and this is made clear by 13:8, which refers to nations rising up against nation, and kingdoms against kingdom, and to earthquakes and famines.[21]

In all this Mark emphasizes God's sovereign rule of history. The expression "nation [will be raised] against nation" may well be a "divine passive" meaning "God will raise up nation against nation."[22] The divine passive was a frequent way by which devout Jews sought to avoid using the sacred name of God.[23] The sovereignty of God over history is also emphasized by the comment, "This must [*dei*] take place" in 13:7b.[24] In a similar way the "must" (*dei*) in 13:10 makes the same point. Although wars and natural disasters must take place, they are not the sign of the end. They must take place, "but the end is still to come" (13:7). The exact referent of the term *end* (*telos*) is debated. It is not a technical term that by itself possesses only a single

---

[19]Beasley-Murray, *Jesus and the Last Days*, p. 394.
[20]Contra Collins, "Eschatological Discourse," p. 1133. There is also no warrant (contra Moloney, *Mark*, p. 255) to see a major shift in 13:7, which describes events before the destruction of Jerusalem, and 13:8, which supposedly describes events after its destruction.
[21]For Old Testament examples of such terminology, cf. Is 19:2; Jer 51:24-58; 2 Chron 15:6. Cf. also 2 Esd 9:1-6; 13:29-32; *T. Jud.* 22:1; *1 Enoch* 99:4; *Sibylline Oracles* 3:635-36; *Jubilees* 11:2; *Apocalypse of Baruch* 70:2-8.
[22]Joel Marcus, *Mark 8–16: A New Translation with Introduction and Commentary*, AYB (New Haven, CT: Yale University Press, 2009), p. 877.
[23]See Robert H. Stein, *The Method and Message of Jesus' Teachings*, rev. ed. (Louisville: Westminster John Knox, 1994), pp. 63-65.
[24]R. T. France, *The Gospel of Mark*, NIGTC (Grand Rapids: Eerdmans, 2002), p. 512, states that the future passive tenses in 13:8 and "this must take place" in 13:7b make the same point—God is in charge. History has not run amok. Cf. Ben Witherington III, *The Gospel of Mark: A Socio-Rhetorical Commentary* (Grand Rapids: Eerdmans, 2001), pp. 343-44; and John R. Donahue and Daniel J. Harrington, *The Gospel of Mark*, SP (Collegeville, MN: Liturgical Press, 2002), p. 369.

meaning. Its specific meaning is determined rather by its use within the context the author gives it. Some suggest it refers to physical death as in 13:12, but it would be strange to claim that physical death (the "end") is not yet in 13:7, and then warn of persecution and physical death in 13:9-13. Another suggestion is that it refers to the claim of the false messiahs and prophets in 13:6-7 who were presumably proclaiming that the end had come.[25] The weakness of this interpretation is that it must presume a referent in their preaching that is not specifically mentioned in 13:6-7. A more common interpretation of the "end" sees it as referring to the end of history in which the full establishment of the kingdom of God takes place by the coming of the Son of Man (cf. 13:24-27, 32-37). Arguing against this interpretation is the fact that no specific mention has been made concerning the parousia in 13:1-7. In fact in the whole discourse of 13:5-23 marked off by the *inclusio* in 13:5 and 23, no explicit mention is made of the parousia. The first clear reference to this is found in 13:24-27, and it is introduced by, "But in those days, after that tribulation [suffering, NRSV]." The most natural referent to "the end" in the expression "the end is still to come" (13:7) is the destruction of the temple, which is the question of the disciples (13:4) that Jesus is answering in 13:5-23. This understanding receives additional support from the fact that 13:5-6 and 13:7-8 are meant to describe what are not the sign of the temple's destruction. They function as "but-the-end-is-not-yet" non-signs of the imminent destruction of Jerusalem.[26] It should be noted that the question of the disciples involves "*the* sign" (singular) when all these things will be, while the potential *signs* suggested in 13:5-13 are all in the plural! When *the* sign appears, it is a single event—the appearance of the abomination of desolation.

In addition to telling the disciples that wars and rumors of wars do not mark the end—that is, the destruction of the temple—Jesus states that wars, earthquakes and famines are only "the beginning of the birth pangs" (13:8b). The exact meaning of the expression "the beginning of the birth pangs" (*archē ōdinōn*) is unclear. At the time Mark wrote, this was not yet a ready-made technical term for the sufferings preceding the coming of the Messiah found

---

[25]Beasley-Murray, *Jesus and the Last Days*, p. 396.
[26]The different meanings of the term *end* in 13:7 and 13 are a good example of how most words possess a semantic range of possible meanings, and that the specific meaning of a word is determined by the context given to it by the author. See Robert H. Stein, *A Basic Guide to Interpreting the Bible: Playing by the Rules*, 2nd ed. (Grand Rapids: Baker Academic, 2011), pp. 49-51.

in later rabbinic thought.²⁷ Its role in 13:9 is unclear. Some argue that it is meant to minimize the events described in 13:7-8. These events are to be understood as only early harbingers of the coming destruction of the temple and Jerusalem, not the finale.²⁸ Others see this as emphasizing the events described in 13:7-8 and point out that these events are indeed the beginning of the birth pains preceding the eschaton.²⁹ The Greek text, itself, permits either interpretation. If, as has been argued, the context of 13:5-13 seeks to define "non-signs" of the coming destruction of Jerusalem, then the former interpretation minimizing the events of 13:7-8 fits this context better. This is further supported by the later revealing of the true sign preceding the destruction of Jerusalem—the appearance of the abomination of desolation (13:14). In the Old Testament the "birth pangs" metaphor is frequently used to describe the tribulation preceding the destruction of a city, and the city most frequently referred to is Jerusalem (Jer 4:31; 6:24; 22:23; 30:6; Is 26:17; Mic 4:9-10). Two other cities in which the "birth pangs" metaphor is used to describe their future destruction are Babylon (Is 13:8; 21:3; Jer 50:43) and Samaria (Hos 13:13).³⁰ The use of this expression with respect to describing the messianic woes preceding the eschaton appears to be later than the time of Mark. Since the expression "birth pangs" is most frequently associated with the destruction of cities and since nothing in 13:1-23 clearly refers to the coming of the Messiah, it is best to interpret this expression with the coming destruction of Jerusalem foretold by Jesus in 13:2, asked about by the disciples in 13:4 and whose twofold question is answered by Jesus in 13:5-23.

Mark 13:9-13—The third non-sign: The mission and persecution of believers. The third non-sign of Jerusalem's imminent destruction is introduced by the second "beware" (*blepete*) in Jesus' discourse (cf. 13:5, 23, here translated "be alert"). It serves both as a warning and an exhortation for the disciples with respect to the persecution they will face. This section is an elaboration of Jesus' earlier teaching in 8:34-38 (cf. also 4:17; 6:11; 10:30) concerning what is entailed in being a follower of Jesus. The encouragement that Jesus gives to his disciples is not that they will escape persecution and

---

²⁷France, *Mark*, pp. 509, 512-13.
²⁸So Beasley-Murray, *Jesus and the Last Days*, p. 397.
²⁹Marcus, *Mark 8–16*, p. 878.
³⁰Timothy C. Gray, *The Temple in the Gospel of Mark: A Study in Its Narrative Role* (Grand Rapids: Baker, 2010), p. 118.

suffering and be "raptured" from it, as the "left behind" theology teaches.[31] It is rather that at such times the Holy Spirit will be present and provide wisdom and encouragement (13:11). In addition Jesus gives the promise that "the one who endures to the end will be saved" (13:13), for "those who lose their life for [Jesus'] sake, and . . . the gospel, will save it" (8:35). The suffering that the disciples would experience was well-known to the readers of Mark, for they knew of various persecutions that the disciples and other followers of Jesus had experienced (cf. Acts 4:1-22; 5:17-18, 27-42; 6:3–7:60; 8:1-3; 9:1-2, 13-16, 23-24; 12:1-5; 14:18; 16:19-40; 18:12-17; 22:30-23:10; 24:1-27; 25:1-12) and from their own experience.[32]

The persecutions described in 13:9 stem from two different sources. One is religious coming from two related Jewish institutions and the other is secular coming from two related governmental sources. The first involves being delivered over for judgment and punishment to councils (*synedria*) and beaten in synagogues (*synagōgas*). The former involves local Jewish community councils[33] in distinction from the Sanhedrin of Jerusalem. Such a council is referred to in Matthew 10:17 (note *councils*, plural) and 5:22 (a local Jewish council). Punishment that the apostles experienced from the Jerusalem Sanhedrin is referred to in Acts 5:27-42; 6:8–7:60. The second Jewish source of judgment and punishment is the local synagogue. The beatings Paul experienced in 2 Corinthians 11:24-25 were probably administered by leaders of local synagogues, and in Acts 22:19 Paul refers to his own actions before his conversion in inflicting such punishment on Christians in the synagogues: "In every synagogue I imprisoned and beat those who believed [in Jesus]." It is clear that Mark is not here addressing his Gentile readers, who had nothing to fear from Jewish councils and syna-

---

[31]For an interesting criticism of the "left behind" theology, see Benjamin L. Merkle, "Who Will Be Left Behind? Rethinking the Meaning of Matthew 24:40-41 and Luke 17:34-35," *WTJ* 72 (2010), pp. 169-79. Merkle argues that being taken away ("raptured") involves being taken away into judgment and being left behind involves being saved from judgment.

[32]If Mark was written to the church in Rome in the late sixties or early seventies, its recipients would have experienced the horrific persecution under Nero. If not, they would have heard of it, unless we date the Gospel earlier.

[33]Although Douglas R. A. Hare, *The Theme of Jewish Persecution of Christians in the Gospel According to St. Matthew*, SNTSMS 6 (New York: Cambridge University Press, 1967), pp. 101-4, argues that these "councils" were probably not Jewish, he can only do so by rejecting the Matthean parallel in 10:17 which refers to "councils [same term as in Mk 13:9]" and floggings they will receive "in *their* [italics added] synagogues."

gogues. Rather, he is reporting to them what Jesus said concerning the persecutions that Peter, James, John, Andrew and his Jewish followers would experience from Jewish councils and synagogues. A mirror reading does not fit well here. Nevertheless, the implication that Mark's readers should be prepared to suffer for the sake of Jesus is self-evident.

A second matching pair of sources for persecution involves being delivered over to governors (*hēgemonōn*) and kings (*basileōn*). Here one thinks of the disciples appearing before governors (Gallio in Acts 18:12-17; Felix in Acts 23:23-24:27; Festus in Acts 24:27-26:32) and kings (Agrippa II in Acts 25:13-26:32). It is assumed that such trials would not be due to wrong doing (1 Pet 4:14-16) but for being a Christian—that is, "because of me" (13:9; cf. 13:13).

Such suffering will serve as a "testimony to them" (13:9). This can be interpreted either positively as "a testimony to them" or negatively as "a testimony against them." Elsewhere in Mark this same expression appears twice more, used negatively in 6:11 and positively in 1:44. The immediate context of 13:9 argues for a positive interpretation here, since the result of this suffering is that the gospel will be proclaimed to all nations. Although certainly not so intended by governors and kings, the persecution of Christians had a serendipitous result.[34] The preposition *eis* in the expression "for a testimony" can be interpreted as introducing either the result or cause of this persecution. The latter interpretation would indicate that ultimately it was God who caused such persecution in order for it to serve as a means of spreading the gospel throughout the world. The former interpretation would indicate that ultimately God is at work in such things for good (Rom 8:28).

Mark 13:10 is considered by most scholars as an editorial comment inserted into the text by the Evangelist.[35] For one, it interrupts the argument in 13:9-13. Its omission would never be missed, for 13:11 flows naturally after 13:9. The style and vocabulary are also very Markan. The term *gospel* (*euangelion*) occurs seven times in Mark (1:1, 14-15, 8:35; 10:29; 13:10; 14:9), and most, if not all, appear to be Markan insertions into the tradition. The term *first* (*prōton*) raises the question, before *what* must the gospel be pro-

---

[34]Note the famous quote of Tertullian in his *Apology* 50, "The blood of the martyrs is the seed of the church."
[35]So Vincent Taylor, *The Gospel According to St. Mark* (London: MacMillan, 1952), p. 507; Hooker, *Mark*, p. 310; Evans, *Mark 8:27–16:20*, p. 310; Stein, *Mark*, p. 600; Marcus, *Mark 8–16*, p. 883.

claimed to all nations? It can be interpreted, "First, before you are arrested, the gospel must be preached to all nations." This, however, loses sight of the context provided in 13:2 and 4 and Jesus' answer to the disciples' question in 13:5-23 that involves the *when* of the coming destruction of Jerusalem and the *sign* preceding this and indicating its imminence. Since the parousia of the Son of Man has not been referred to up to this point in Mark 13 and will only be mentioned later in 13:24-27 and 32-37, it is unlikely that Mark intends "first" to be understood as "[But before the coming of the Son of Man] the good news must first be proclaimed to all nations." Thus the temporal "first" is best interpreted "[But] first [before the destruction of Jerusalem] the gospel must be proclaimed to all the nations."

The concern that the gospel must be preached to all the nations is found scattered throughout the New Testament.[36] It was already taking place during Jesus' ministry (5:1-20; 7:24-31; cf. 3:8; 11:17; 14:9; cf. Mt 28:19-20). There is a sense in which Paul saw this as already an accomplished reality in his ministry, for he could say that the gospel was "now disclosed, and . . . made known to all the Gentiles" (Rom 16:26) and "bearing fruit and growing in the whole world" (Col 1:6; cf. also Col 1:26; Rom 1:5, 8; 10:18; 15:19, 23). We must remember that in seeking to understand what Mark means by 13:10, we cannot bring in at this point present-day missiological language such as "unreached people groups" to understand 13:10. For Mark "all nations" meant the Roman world and its neighbors, and by the time Mark wrote his Gospel there was a sense that the gospel had been made known to all these nations.[37]

To those being brought to trial for his sake (13:9), Jesus gives the promise that the Holy Spirit would be present to give wisdom and even the words to say at their defense (13:11). This brings to mind Peter and John, "uneducated and ordinary men" (Acts 4:13) but "filled with the Holy Spirit" (Acts 4:8), who at their trial astonished the religious leaders by the wisdom and power with which they spoke. It also recalls God's enabling Moses to speak to Pharaoh (Ex 4:10-17), the equipping of the prophet Jeremiah for his ministry (Jer 1:6-10) and the various times in Acts when believers were filled with the

---

[36]For the Old Testament interest in outreach to Gentiles, cf. Is 42:6-7; 49:6, 12; 52:10; 56:1-8; 60:1-16; Ps 96 among others. It should also be remembered that part of the temple involved the Court of the Gentiles.

[37]So France, *Mark*, pp. 516-17.

Spirit while speaking (e.g., Acts 2:14-17; 4:8, 31; 6:8-10; 7:55; 8:29-35; 13:9-10). For the majority of the church who were uneducated and powerless (1 Cor 1:26), this promise provided encouragement and assurance that they would not stand alone in their defense before powerful judges and rulers. The Holy Spirit would be present, guiding them in what to say. Thus they did not need to be anxious in such circumstances.[38]

In the concluding two verses of this section the persecution reaches a crescendo of horrors. Jesus warns the disciples that they will not only face hostile councils, synagogues, governors, kings and beatings, but they will experience hostility from their own families. This is portrayed by an escalation of family hostility involving brothers toward each other, fathers toward their own children and children toward their fathers. What is portrayed here is not the murdering of one family member by another but the betrayal of a family member who is a believer by another who is not to hostile authorities, resulting in the believer's death (Mt 10:21; 10:34-39/Lk 12:52-53).[39]

The result, Jesus says, is that "you will be hated by all because of my name" (13:13; cf. Jn 15:18-19). Mark probably did not mean that every human being will hate those who follow him, but rather that all elements of society, whether ruler or ruled, educated or uneducated, literate or illiterate, powerful or weak, judges or criminals, even one's own family, will hate those who bear the name "Christian."[40] Despite such great hostility and the bleak outlook for a peaceful life, Jesus ends Mark 13:9-13 with the promise that "the one who endures to the end will be saved." Whereas in 13:7 the term *end*

---

[38]Taylor, *Mark*, p. 508, rightly points out that what is prohibited is not thinking about what to say but being anxious over it. It should also be noted that this promise is not directed to preachers with respect to their ministry of proclaiming the gospel. It is rather a promise given to those on trial facing possible martyrdom for their faith in Jesus Christ.

[39]For Old Testament examples of such internecine, domestic hostility, see Is 19:2; Ezek 38:21; Mic 7:6. For other examples in contemporary Jewish literature of the times, see Evans, *Mark 8:27-16:20*, p. 312. A similar family experience of a Gentile converting to Judaism is found in *Joseph and Aseneth* 11:4-6: "All people have come to hate me, / and on top of those my father and my mother, / because I, too, have come to hate their gods.... / And therefore my father and my mother and my whole family / have come to hate me and said, 'Aseneth is not our daughter / because she destroyed our gods.' / And all people hate me.... / And now, in this humiliation of mine, all have (come to) hate me, / And gloat over this affliction of mine." James H. Charlesworth, ed., *The Old Testament Pseudepigrapha*, ABRL (New York: Doubleday, 1985), 2:218.

[40]The name "Christian" postdates the ministry of Jesus (Acts 11:26). In 13:13 the expression "because of my name" is used. Elsewhere in Mark we come across the expressions "because of me" (13:9), "for my sake, and for the sake of the gospel" (8:35) and "ashamed of me and of my words" (8:38).

(*telos*) refers to the destruction of Jerusalem, here it refers to the end of one's life. To those enduring in faithfulness unto death, Jesus promises the gift of eternal life and entrance into the kingdom of God (14:25).[41]

Mark 13:14-20: The Sign of the Abomination of Desolation Heralding the Temple's and Jerusalem's Imminent Destruction and the Warning to Flee Judea

This section is intimately tied to the preceding section both thematically and literarily. It continues the answer of Jesus to the disciples' questions as to the forthcoming destruction of the temple (13:4). It is also connected to 13:5-13 by the third "when" (*hotan*; cf. 13:7, 11, 14). However, there is a major change in Jesus' teaching concerning the destruction of the temple and Jerusalem. In 13:5-13 the disciples are warned not to mistake various events such as the appearing of false messianic claimants, wars and rumors of wars, and persecution as "the sign" of Jerusalem's imminent destruction. When these events take place, they are told, "do not be alarmed" (13:7) and "do not worry beforehand" (13:11), for these are not "the sign."[42] Now, conversely, they are told to be alarmed and "flee" (13:14).[43] "Until now, the message has been 'Wait! Do not be overwhelmed. Endure!' But now the time for action has arrived."[44] Furthermore, the sign asked for in 13:4 is now given—the appearance of the "[abomination of desolation] set up where it ought not to be." Unlike the various events referred to in 13:5-13 that stand in contrast with the singular sign referred to in 13:4, the abomination of desolation is singular in nature, and the visual nature of the sign's appearance (when you

---

[41]For a similar promise, compare 2 Esd 6:25, "It shall be that whoever remains after all that I have foretold to you shall be saved and shall see my salvation and the end of my world."

[42]Eckhard Schnabel, *40 Questions About the End Times* (Grand Rapids: Kregel, 2011), pp. 31-43, argues that Jesus spoke of eleven signs that would herald the end of the age. Based primarily on his interpretation of Matthew 24, these involve (1) seduction, messianic pretenders; (2) wars, rumors of war, international unrest; (3) famines; (4) earthquakes; (5) persecution; (6) false prophets; (7) injustice, lack of love; (8) universal proclamation of the gospel; (9) the destruction of Jerusalem; (10) messianic pretenders, false prophets; and (11) the return of Jesus. Yet the only sign referred to in Mark 13 is "the" sign asked about in 13:4 and described in 13:14, and this involves not the end of the age, but the end of the temple and Jerusalem (13:7). Schnabel does agree, however, that the ninth sign, the destruction of the temple, was fulfilled in A.D. 66-70.

[43]Adela Y. Collins, "The Apocalyptic Rhetoric of Mark 13 in Historical Context," *Biblical Research* 41:21.

[44]Hooker, *Mark*, p. 313; cf. also Adela Y. Collins, *Mark: A Commentary*, Hermeneia (Minneapolis: Fortress, 2007), p. 607.

"see")⁴⁵ is emphasized. The response is also emphasized, "then . . . flee," as the following verses indicate (13:14b-16). The scene of the appearance of the abomination of desolation is singular as well. It takes place "where he ought not to be"—that is, in the temple in Jerusalem—as the Feast of Hanukkah teaches. This sign would appear not in a distant place from which wars and rumors of wars come or where Christians will appear before councils, synagogues, governors and kings in the proclamation of the gospel to all nations, but in the temple in Jerusalem.

The parenthetical comment "let the reader understand" is best understood as a Markan insertion into the tradition directed to the readers of his Gospel.⁴⁶ The addition of such parenthetical comments is a Markan characteristic, as can be seen in 1:34d; 2:10; 3:30; 7:11, 19. Attempts to interpret this as a statement of Jesus addressed to his disciples are unconvincing due to the reference to the "reader" (Jesus' disciples would have been referred to as hearers) and the use of the third person singular ("let the reader") instead of the second person plural ("disciples").⁴⁷ Where Jesus does use the third person in addressing his disciples or audience, he uses "Let anyone with ears to hear listen" and its variations (Mk 4:9, 23; 8:18; Mt 11:15; 13:9, 15 [2x], 16, 43; Lk 8:8; 9:44; 14:35; cf. also Rev 2:7, 11, 17, 29; 3:6, 13, 22; 13:9). Outside of Mark 13:14 and its parallel in Matthew 24:15, the only other place in the New Testament where a "reader" is referred to is Revelation 1:3.

As to the identification of the reader being addressed by Mark, two possibilities present themselves. One possibility is that it is directed to the specific individual reading the Gospel aloud to its intended audience. The other is that "the reader" refers to the recipients to whom the Gospel was sent—that is, the particular Christian community to whom the Evangelist

---

⁴⁵Hengel, *Studies in the Gospel of Mark*, p. 19. Cf. also Hooker (*Mark*, pp. 302, 313), who points out that the appearance of the abomination of desolation in 13:14a points to a particular event, not to a series of events as in 13:5-13.

⁴⁶So, among others, William L. Lane, *The Gospel According to Mark*, NICNT (Grand Rapids: Eerdmans, 1974), p. 467; Hooker, *Mark*, p. 314; Adela Y. Collins, *The Beginning of the Gospel: Probings of Mark in Context* (Minneapolis: Fortress, 1992), pp. 85-86; Collins, "Apocalyptic Rhetoric," pp. 22, 25; Evans, *Mark 8:27-16:20*, p. 320.

⁴⁷Contra Brant Pitre, *Jesus, the Tribulation, and the End of the Exile: Restoration Eschatology and the Origin of the Atonement* (Grand Rapids: Baker, 2005), pp. 309-13. Contrast, however, Robert Fowler's summary of the general consensus in *Let the Reader Understand: Reader-Response Criticism and the Gospel of Mark* (Minneapolis: Augsburg, 1991), p. 83: "The parenthesis makes no sense at all as a statement by Jesus."

wrote. The latter is more likely, since Mark wrote his Gospel not for the individual who would perform the actual reading but for his intended audience. These "hearers" would in fact be the "readers" of the Gospel. Here one should compare Acts 15:31 where the Christian community is referred to as having "read" the letter from Jerusalem and having rejoiced on reading it, even though it was no doubt read to them and they "heard" its content. We find a similar instance in 2 Corinthians 1:13 where the Corinthian church is referred to as having "read" and understood Paul's earlier letter, even though they also no doubt "heard" Paul's letter read to them. In Ephesians 3:4 Paul's hearers are referred to as "reading" the letter: "When you [plural] read this" (RSV), and in Colossians 4:16 Paul tells the Colossians that they [plural] should read the letter from Laodicea. Consequently, the address to the reader in 13:14 would have probably been understood by those hearing the Gospel read to them as being addressed to them, and not only the actual reader. Thus those "hearing" the Gospel were in fact the "readers" of Mark's Gospel.

As to what the readers/hearers of Mark are supposed to understand, this is debated. Some suggest it is to alert the readers that the abomination of desolation would resemble what is described in Daniel 9:27; 11:31; 12:5-13. Others suggest that the readers should note that a masculine participle ("standing") is used to define the neuter noun "abomination of desolation" (ESV); indicating that the abomination of desolation is a person, not a thing.[48] Still another suggestion is that Mark is telling his readers that the abomination of desolation should be interpreted not simply in light of Daniel but even more so in light of the appearance of the abomination of desolation in 167 B.C. as recorded in 1 Maccabees 1:20-4:61 and 2 Maccabees 6:1-10:8.[49]

Whereas the expression "the abomination of desolation" is somewhat ambiguous to most Christian readers today, it would not have been so to Jesus' disciples and for many of the readers of Mark. Those familiar with the book of Daniel would be aware that this expression was found in several

---

[48]Gundry, *Mark*, p. 742; cf. Larry Perkins, "'Let the Reader Understand': A Contextual Interpretation of Mark 13:14," *BBR* 16, no. 1 (2006): 103n22: "The use of the masculine participle to define a neuter noun in 13:14 may be precisely why Jesus warns the reader . . . to understand what the prophecy is truly describing."

[49]So Moloney, *Mark*, p. 259. For additional suggestions, see Gray, *Temple in the Gospel of Mark*, pp. 130-32.

places in the book: 9:27 ("and in their place shall be an abomination that desolates, until the decreed end is poured out upon the desolator"); 11:31 ("They shall . . . set up the abomination that makes desolate"); and 12:11 ("and the abomination that desolates is set up"). In the Greek translation of the Old Testament called the Septuagint (LXX), which was the Bible of most of Mark's readers, the Greek expression in Daniel 12:11 is exactly the same as that used in Mark 13:14: *to bdelugma tēs erēmōseōs*. In Daniel 9:27 we find *bdelugma* and the plural *tōn erēmōseōv*, and in Daniel 11:31 we find *bdelugma erēmōseōs*.

We find an interesting parallel to the coming destruction of Jerusalem in Ezekiel 8–9.[50] There the sins and "abominations" of Israel are described as the cause of the coming destruction of Jerusalem and the temple in 587 B.C. The profaning of the temple is not seen as a future action of the nation of Babylon and king Nebuchadnezzar but rather as due to Israel's abominable acts. These included massive idolatry (8:1-6); the worship of animals (8:7-13); the worship of Tammuz, the Mesopotamian god of vegetation (8:14-15); and murder and injustice (9:9). Far from being the cause of the abominations occurring in the temple, the Babylonians would be God's instrument of judgment against Israel's abominations. Jesus likewise prophesied to the people of Israel that the temple would be destroyed because of their sins, which included profaning the temple (Mk 11:15-17), rejecting the coming of God's Son (12:1-12), ignoring the coming of the Son of God and their day of visitation (Mt 23:37/Lk 13:34), making life difficult for the people (Mt 23:4), religious chicanery and concentrating on religious trivia while ignoring justice and mercy (Mt 23:23), religious hypocrisy (Mt 23:25-28), and so on. In 587 B.C. it was not a foreign nation that profaned the temple, but Israel. Likewise in A.D. 70 it would not be a foreign nation that would profane the temple, but Israel again. Furthermore, just as Babylonia in the former instance served as God's instrument of judgment in destroying Jerusalem and the temple, so Rome would be God's instrument in the latter instance.

We should not confuse, however, the abomination of desolation in 13:14 with the "abominations" (plural) of Israel referred to in Ezekiel 8–9. For one, the terminology is different. In Ezekiel 8:6 (2x), 9, 13, 15, 17 the term *abomi-*

---

[50]This was brought to my attention by my colleague and friend Dr. Daniel Block.

nations is in the Hebrew Old Testament *tô ʿēbôt* and in the LXX *anomia*. In Daniel the term used for "abomination" in the Hebrew Old Testament is *šiqqûṣ* and in the LXX *bdelugma*. In addition it should be noted that the term in Ezekiel is always plural, whereas in the two main references in Daniel 11:31 and 12:11 the term is singular. Most importantly we should note that whereas in Ezekiel 8–9 the abominations are the cause of God's judgment of Jerusalem by Babylon in 587 B.C., the abomination of desolation in Mark 13:14 is not the cause of God's destruction of Jerusalem in A.D. 70. It is rather the *sign* of the imminence of its coming.

For the disciples of Jesus and the Jewish readers of Mark, and for observant Jews ever since, the yearly, eight-day celebration of the Festival of Lights[51] recalls the cleansing and rededication of the temple in 164 B.C.[52] This was accomplished by the Maccabees (1 Macc 4:36-59; 2 Macc 1:18) and undid the abomination of desolation that occurred three years earlier when Antiochus Epiphanes polluted and desecrated the temple. The exact nature of the abomination of desolation is uncertain. Some suggest that it was the erection of an altar to Zeus on the altar of burnt offering in the temple (1 Macc 1:54; 6:7). Another suggestion is that it involved the sacrificing of an abominable offering, probably swine, on the altar of burnt offering (1 Macc 1:47, 59; 2 Macc 6:5; cf. also *Ant.* 12.254; *J.W.* 1.34). Still another suggestion is that it was a combination of the above. Regardless of the exact nature of the abomination of desolation that occurred in 167 B.C., it was clearly a horrific and sacrilegious act that was part of Antiochus Epiphanes's attempt to destroy the Jewish religion (1 Macc 1:41-64). For the disciples of Jesus their understanding of the "abomination of desolation" did not come primarily from a personal study of Ezekiel 8–9 or Daniel 11–12. It came rather from the yearly celebration of the eight-day festival of Hanukkah or Feast of Lights, just as even today in a much more literate society the understanding of Christmas is more influenced by the yearly rituals associated with this festival than by a personal reading of Matthew 1–2 and Luke 1–2.

---

[51]There are a number of terms and expressions used to describe this festival: (1) Feast of Dedication (1 Macc 4:56, 59; 2 Macc 2:9, 19; Jn 10:22); (2) Feast of Purification (2 Macc 2:16, 18; 10:3, 5); (3) Feast of Tabernacles/Booths (2 Macc 1:9, 18); (4) Feast of Lights (*Ant.* 2.325; *b. B. Qam.* 6.6).

[52]"Every Jew of Mark's day knew about Antiochus Epiphanes and his blasphemous acts: The Festival of Dedication ensured that" (Beasley-Murray, *Jesus and the Last Days*, p. 219).

As to how Mark and the Jesus of Mark's Gospel understood the future abomination of desolation mentioned in 13:14, there have been a number of suggestions. Some of the more important are:

1. The attempt by Caligula in A.D. 39-40 to erect a statue of himself in the temple of Jerusalem. Because of fear that this might result in a major revolt by the Jews, it was never carried out. Nevertheless this caused great consternation and turmoil in Judea (*Ant.* 18.261-309).[53]

2. The attempt by Pontius Pilate, also not carried out, to have Roman soldiers enter into Jerusalem ostentatiously displaying their military standards that Jews considered blasphemous (*Ant.* 18.55-59; *J.W.* 2.169-74).

3. The atrocities committed by the Zealots under the leadership of John of Gischala and Eleazar, the son of Simon, and their investiture of Phanni as high priest in A.D. 67-68 (*J.W.* 4.147-57; 4.160).[54]

4. The role of Titus in the destruction of Jerusalem and his forceful entrance into the most sacred part of the temple sanctuary in A.D. 70 (*J.W.* 6.260).[55]

5. The Roman soldiers setting up their standards in the temple and sacrificing to them as they proclaimed Titus "emperor" (*J.W.* 6.316). The masculine "he" ("where *he* ought not to be") is understood as referring to the man behind the act.[56]

6. The events leading up to the siege of Jerusalem by the Roman army in A.D. 70.[57]

---

[53]So T. W. Manson, *The Sayings of Jesus as Recorded in the Gospels According to St. Matthew and St. Luke: Arranged with Introduction and Commentary* (Grand Rapids: Eerdmans, 1957), pp. 329-30; Lloyd Gaston, *No Stone on Another: Studies in the Significance of the Fall of Jerusalem in the Synoptic Gospels* (Leiden: Brill, 1970), pp. 25-27; N. H. Taylor, "Palestinian Christianity and the Caligula Crisis Part II: The Markan Eschatological Discourse," *JSNT* 62 (1996): 20-21.

[54]So Joel Marcus, "The Jewish War and the *Sitz im Leben* of Mark," *JBL* 111 (1992): 454-56; Witherington, *Mark*, pp. 345-46.

[55]So Dieter Lührmann, *Das Markusevangelium*, HZNT 3 (Tübingen: Mohr Siebeck, 1987), pp. 221-22; Hooker, *Mark*, p. 314; W. A. Such, *The Abomination of Desolation in the Gospel of Mark: Its Historical Reference in Mark 13:14 and Its Impact in the Gospel* (Lanham, MD: University Press of America, 1999), pp. 96-102, 206; Moloney, *Mark*, pp. 259-60.

[56]So Desmond Ford, *The Abomination of Desolation in Biblical Eschatology* (Washington, DC: University Press of America, 1979), p. 158.

[57]So Ezra Palmer Gould, *A Critical and Exegetical Commentary on the Gospel According to St. Mark*, ICC (New York: T & T Clark, 1896), pp. 246-47; Ford, *Abomination of Desolation*, pp. 166-69.

7. The destruction of the temple in Jerusalem by the Roman army.[58]
8. A future event involving the antichrist and preceding the parousia (2 Thess 2:3-4).[59]

In seeking to evaluate the various suggestions as to the referent of the expression "the abomination of desolation," the literary and historical contexts place several restraints on any interpretation of what Mark means by this expression.[60] These require that:

- The abomination of desolation must have some interpretative continuity with Daniel 9:25-27; 11:29-35; 12:1-13; 1 Maccabees 1:54, 59, where the expression "abomination of desolation" is used, and with the yearly celebration of the Feast of Lights in Israel. This would be the linguistic and historical context within which Jesus and the disciples, and Mark and his readers, would have interpreted the expression. The context centers on the temple in Jerusalem, its altar and its ritual sacrifices.
- The sign of the abomination of desolation must be sufficiently recognizable that it could warn those living in Judea and Jerusalem to flee the coming destruction of the city and the temple.
- The sign of the abomination of desolation must occur before the Roman armies had surrounded the city of Jerusalem and laid siege to it, for after this there would be no possibility of flight for those in Judea and Jerusalem.
- The masculine participle "standing" indicates that the abomination of desolation probably refers to a person, rather than a "thing."

With respect to the first two suggested explanations of the abomination of desolation, it should be noted that both these events occurred over two decades too early to serve as a sign for the imminent destruction of Jerusalem. In the mind of Mark's readers the warning to flee Judea and Jerusalem involved the nearness of the city's destruction. The appearance of the "sign" and warnings to flee immediately (13:15-16) would not have been understood

---

[58]So Rudolf Pesch, *Das Markusevangelium, Part 2: Kommentur zu 8,27–16,20*, 2nd ed., HTKNT (Freiburg: Herder, 1981), p. 292.
[59]So Taylor, *Mark*, p. 511; C. E. B. Cranfield, *The Gospel According to Mark*, CGTC (New York: Cambridge University Press, 1959), pp. 402-3; Evans, *Mark 8:27–16:20*, p. 320; James R. Edwards, *The Gospel According to Mark*, PNTC (Grand Rapids: Eerdmans, 2002), pp. 398-99.
[60]See France, *Mark*, p. 520.

as involving a sign, a delay of the flight for over two decades,[61] and a flight from Jerusalem around A.D. 67-69. This indicates that the interpretations of the "abomination of desolation" in options 1 and 2 would not have been interpreted by Mark's readers as a sign of the imminent destruction of Jerusalem and the need for immediate flight from the area decades before A.D. 70. As to explanations 4, 5 and 7, these events would have been too late to serve as a sign to flee Jerusalem.[62] These all presume a time after the siege of Jerusalem, when flight was no longer possible, and the Jews within the city were either killed or led off into slavery. The abomination of desolation must involve a desecration that preceded the siege and fall of Jerusalem. It should be remembered that the prior abomination of desolation in 167 B.C. involved the defiling of the temple not its destruction, and the annual festival of Hanukkah celebrated the cleansing of the temple not its rebuilding. Explanation 6 is unconvincing because it refers to a "thing," whereas the abomination of desolation refers to a person, as the masculine participle "standing" indicates.[63] Thus the abomination of desolation cannot refer to a thing, such as the events leading up to the siege of Jerusalem, but must refer in some way to a person. Concerning explanation 8, the future persecution and horrors associated with the appearance of the antichrist will not be limited to Judea and Jerusalem, successful flight will not be possible, and the time of the year will be irrelevant (13:18).

The best interpretation of the abomination of desolation is explanation 3. This involves the actions of the Zealots and their leaders, John of Gischala and Eleazar in A.D. 67-68,[64] who were involved in numerous sacrilegious actions within the temple. This included internecine warfare with other

---

[61]The book of Acts assumes the continued presence of the church in Jerusalem at least until the end of the events recorded in Acts 28:30-31, which took place around A.D. 62.

[62]Marcus, *Mark 8-16*, p. 890, rightly points out, "What sense does it make to enjoin flight to the mountains (13:14c) when the Temple and the capital city have already been destroyed and the war effectively lost?"

[63]The Greek participle *hestēkota* is a masculine singular accusative. The neuter singular accusative would be *hestēkos*.

[64]So Witherington, *Mark*, p. 345; Marcus, *Mark 8-16*, pp. 890-91. R. S. Snow, "Let the Reader Understand: Mark's Use of Jeremiah 7 in Mark 13:14," *BBR* 21 (2011): 467-77, argues that the abomination of desolation was "the corrupt and fraudulent activity of the temple leaders." However, such activity was already true during the ministry of Jesus as his "cleansing of the temple" indicates. Something more specific is required as a sign to flee immediately from Jerusalem. The culmination of such corruption of the temple leaders led to the abomination of desolation—the investing of Phanni as high priest—despite his being unqualified for this role.

Jewish leaders and groups, but it was probably their investing Phanni in the temple as high priest, even though he was not of high priestly descent and was mentally defective, that was the abomination (*J.W.* 4.151-57). This interpretation sees the abomination of desolation not as the destroyer of the temple (i.e., Titus) or the disaster itself (i.e., the destruction of the temple and Jerusalem), but the sign of the coming disaster (i.e., the installation of Phanni as high priest, as a pawn for the Zealots and their activities). The appearance of the abomination of desolation is clearly distinguished by Mark from the appearance of false christs and messianic pretenders.

Whereas "the reader" of Mark is exhorted to understand the "sign" of the abomination of desolation, the exhortation addressed to those who actually see this sign involves the disciples (13:1-5a),[65] and by implication the followers of Jesus in Judea: "then those in Judea must flee to the mountains" (13:14c). This injunction makes good sense when applied to the followers of Jesus in Judea, but not when applied to the readers of Mark. Here the author of the Gospel is reporting the Jesus traditions concerning the fall of Jerusalem to his readers. Why he is doing so and what the implications of this may be for his readers who do not reside in Judea will be discussed below in the summary of our discussion of Mark 13:14-23, but Mark is reporting at this point Jesus' instructions to his followers in Judea for the time when the abomination of desolation would appear in the temple of Jerusalem. He does not intend that his readers understand this warning as a literal instruction that they are to follow. He indicates this clearly to his non-Judean readers by defining the audience to which the command is directed as "those in Judea" (13:14c)!

The command to "flee" Judea is not a figurative call to abandon Judaism either in the original situation of Jesus or that of Mark.[66] The command is to be understood literally as referring to the land of Judea, just as in every other instance the term appears in Mark (1:5; 3:7; 10:1), even if the specific examples given in 13:16-17 use exaggerated language. The command to flee Jerusalem recalls similar exhortations such as:

---

[65]Compare Moloney, *Mark*, p. 273, who states, "Jesus' discourse on the end of Jerusalem and the end of the world is aimed at the disciples."
[66]Contra Werner H. Kelber, *The Kingdom in Mark: A New Place and a New Time* (Philadelphia: Fortress, 1974), p. 121.

Flee for safety, O children of Benjamin,
from the midst of Jerusalem!
Blow the trumpet in Tekoa,
and raise a signal on Beth-haccherem;
for evil looms out of the north,
and great destruction. (Jer 6:1)

Then Mattathias cried out in the town with a loud voice, saying: "Let every one who is zealous for the law and supports the covenant come out with me!" Then he and his sons fled to the hills and left all that they had in the town. (1 Macc 2:27-28; cf. also Rev 18:4)

Such exhortations make perfectly good sense and should not be "de-historized." The exhortation to flee Judea is especially appropriate in light of the tendency to seek safety and security from the Roman invasion (cf. *J.W.* 4.106-11, 121-25, 135-37) within the mighty fortress of Jerusalem (cf. Ps 48:12-14) and the sanctity of God's temple (Ps 48:8-9).

The first imperative given in response to the appearance of the sign of the abomination of desolation has often been associated with an oracle preceding the destruction of Jerusalem that led Jewish Christians to flee to the city of Pella for safety (Eusebius, *Ecclesiastical History* 3.5.3; Epiphanius, *Panarion* or *Refutation of Heresies* 29.7.7-8; 30.2.7; *Treatise on Weights and Measures* 15).[67] Some scholars see Mark 13:14-16 as this oracle,[68] but the majority

---

[67] "The people of the church in Jerusalem were commanded by an oracle given by revelation before the war to those in the city who were worthy of it to depart and dwell in one of the cities of Perea which they called Pella. To it those who believed on Christ migrated from Jerusalem" (Eusebius, *Ecclesiastical History*, vol. 1, trans. Kirsopp Lake, Loeb Classical Library [Cambridge, MA: Harvard University Press], p. 201). "Since all the disciples had settled in Pella after they left Jerusalem—Christ told them to abandon Jerusalem and withdraw from it because of its coming siege. And they settled in Peraea for this reason and . . . spent their lives there" (Frank Williams, *The Panarion of Epiphanius of Salamis* [Leiden: Brill, 1987], p. 118). "For when the city [of Jerusalem] was about to be taken and destroyed by the Romans, it was revealed in advance to all the disciples by an angel of God that they should remove from the city, as it was going to be completely destroyed. They sojourned as emigrants in Pella . . . in Transjordan. And this city is said to be of the Decapolis" (J. E. Dean, ed., *Epiphanius's Treatise on Weights and Measures: Syriac Version*, Studies in Ancient Oriental Civilization 11 [Chicago: University of Chicago Press, 1935], p. 31).

[68] So Sidney Sowers, "The Circumstances and Recollection of the Pella Flight," *Theologische Zeitschrift* 26 (1970): 305-20; Lane, *Mark*, p. 468; Pesch, *Markusevangelium*, pp. 292-95; Vicky Balabanski, *Eschatology in the Making: Mark, Matthew, and the Didache*, SNTSMS 97 (New York: Cambridge University Press, 1997), pp. 101-34; Moloney, *Mark*, pp. 260-63.

argue against this.[69] The main argument against such an association is that a flight to Pella hardly corresponds to a flight to the mountains, since Pella was a major city in the Decapolis in the Jordan valley. Nevertheless it is unlikely that the tradition of the Jewish Christian community having fled Jerusalem shortly before its destruction is a later *de novo* invention of the early church. Something like Mark 13:14-16 and an actual flight from Jerusalem before its destruction in A.D. 70 most likely lies behind this tradition.

The other two imperatives ("the one on the housetop must not go down or enter the house to take anything away" in 13:15, and "the one in the field must not turn back to get a coat" in 13:16) emphasize the necessity of immediate flight from the city. Their exaggerated nature urges flight without delay. In actuality the approach of the Roman army would not involve "Blitzkieg" warfare, but rather would involve a steady, methodological and crushing advance toward Jerusalem eliminating any areas of resistance on the way. Thus there would be time for those relaxing on the rooftops to come down, gather certain necessary items and leave the city. Similarly, the person in the field could return to his home to retrieve his coat, but they should by no means play a waiting game. They should leave Judea quickly while the "getting was good"!

The description of the horror surrounding the coming destruction of Jerusalem in 13:17-20 gives the reason why fleeing the city immediately is necessary. The plight of the most vulnerable, those pregnant and nursing their children,[70] is described with a "woe"[71] or "alas," due to the additional burdens and limitations their conditions bring. This is followed by a prayer that the coming flight not be in the winter, when the cold and flooding wadis and the muddy paths would make travel more difficult and hazardous. The reference to "in those days" (*en ekeinais tais hēmerais*) should not be understood as a technical term for the "last days,"[72] for everywhere else in Mark the expression is used as a reference to an event that took place in the time of Jesus (1:9; 8:1; cf. 4:35; cf. also, e.g., Mt 3:1; Lk 2:1; 4:2; 5:35; 9:36). Thus there

---

[69] Beasley-Murray, *Jesus and the Last Days*, pp. 412-13; Evans, *Mark 8:27–16:20*, p. 320; France, *Mark*, p. 526.
[70] Cf. 2 Kings 8:12; 15:16; Hos 13:16; Amos 1:13.
[71] For other examples of prophetic "woes," cf. Is 3:11; 28:1; 29:1, 15; 30:1; 31:1; 33:1; Jer 4:13; 13:27; Ezek 13:18; Hos 7:13; 9:12; Amos 5:18.
[72] Contra Edwards, *Mark*, p. 400.

is no reason to interpret this phrase eschatologically ("when history as we know it comes to an end"). It should rather be interpreted prophetically ("in those days when Jerusalem will be destroyed").

The degree of destruction described in 13:19 ("there will be suffering, such as has not been from the beginning of the creation that God created until now, no, and never will be") has led some to interpret this as a reference to the great tribulation and the coming of the antichrist before the parousia. Others have interpreted the tribulation described in 13:19-20 as referring to the present experience of Christians at the time of Mark's writing his Gospel.[73] Such a mirror reading of this passage, however, "would appear to be an example of overzealous application of the redaction-critical principle that every word of the Gospels must be related to the situation of the readers."[74] In the text it is evident that Jerusalem and believers in Judea are in mind, and there is no hint that Mark has changed his focus to the Roman or Gentile world. The wording of 13:19 is furthermore best understood as involving hyperbolic language that over time had become an idiom. This can be seen in the following passages:

> I will cause the heaviest hail to fall that *has ever* fallen in Egypt from the day it was founded *until now*. (Ex 9:18, italics added)

> Then there will be a loud cry throughout the whole land of Egypt, such as *has never been or will ever be again*. (Ex 11:6, italics added)

> For the day of the LORD is coming; it is near—
> a day of darkness and gloom,
> a day of clouds and thick darkness!
> Like blackness spread upon the mountains
> a great and powerful army comes;
> their like *has never been from of old*,
> nor will be again after them *in ages to come*. (Joel 2:1-2, italics added)[75]

Thus it is best to understand 13:19 as using impressionistic, hyperbolic language to describe the terrible, horrific suffering and tribulation that would fall on those in Judea and Jerusalem who do not flee the coming Roman

---

[73]Rudolf Pesch, *Naherwartungen: Tradition und Redaktion in Mk 13*, KBANT (Düsseldorf: Patmos, 1968), pp. 151-54.
[74]Beasley-Murray, *Jesus and the Last Days*, p. 418.
[75]Cf. also Deut 4:32; Dan 12:1; 1 Macc 9:27; *Assumption of Moses* 8:1; 1QM 1:11-12; Rev 16:18.

army, its destruction of the city and the bloodthirsty sword of its legions.[76] The concluding phrase, "and never will be," is probably best understood as assuming that time will continue after that tribulation,[77] but there is no indication of how long "after that tribulation" (13:24 ESV) the coming of the Son of Man (13:24-27) will be.

A second, general description of the horrific nature of the tribulation that will take place when the temple and Jerusalem are destroyed is given in 13:20. Continuing the hyperbolic language of the previous verse, Jesus states that "if the Lord had not cut short those days, no one would be saved" (lit. "all flesh would not be saved"). "Saved" here refers to physically surviving the siege and destruction of Jerusalem (cf. 3:4; 5:23; 15:30-31). It is not "unbridled hyperbole" to see this verse as involving the destruction of the temple and Jerusalem in A.D. 70,[78] but taking seriously the context in which the statement is found (13:2, 4, 14) that refers to the destruction of the temple and Jerusalem.

> It is evident that Jerusalem and the Jews in Judea are in mind in vv. 14-18, without reference to Christians in Rome or anywhere else in the gentile world; it would be unreasonable to leap from Judea and its people in vv. 14-18 to Rome and its Christians in vv. 19-20 without any hint of a change of subjects, or place or time.... Similar considerations apply to the notion that vv. 19-20 advance from the situation of the Jews in Palestine to a worldwide tribulation in the last days.[79]

The Lord, however, will "cut short those [lit. *the*] days" to permit the survival of a remnant. He will do this for the sake of his "elect." The redundant Semiticisms ("from the beginning of the *creation* that God *created*" [13:19] and "for the sake of his *elect*, whom he *chose*" [lit. *elected*—13:20]) should be noted.[80] Some argue that these are indicators of the saying's authenticity, but it should be noted that redundancy is a characteristic of Markan style.[81]

---

[76]For the use of overstatement and hyperbole in the Bible, see Stein, *Basic Guide*, pp. 174-88.
[77]Lane, *Mark*, p. 472.
[78]Contra Evans, *Mark 8:27–16:20*, p. 322.
[79]Beasley-Murray, *Jesus and the Last Days*, p. 418.
[80]For other examples in Mark of what appears to be Semitic redundancy, see 2:19-20 (bridegroom/bridegroom); 4:30 (compare/parable); 7:13 (tradition/handed on [same Greek root]); 11:28 (authority/authority); 12:14 (sincere/truth [same Greek root]); 12:23-25 (resurrection/when they rise [same Greek root]—there is a textual problem here).
[81]See Robert H. Stein, "Duality in Mark," in *New Studies in the Synoptic Problem: Oxford Conference, April 2008*, ed. P. Foster et al., BETL 239 (Leuven: Peeters, 2011), pp. 253-80.

The idea of God shortening the days for the sake of his people is found frequently in Jewish literature.[82] The beneficiary of God's gracious act of shortening those days is the "elect" (13:20; cf. also 22, 27).[83] Within the present context the "elect" refers to God's people trapped in Jerusalem during the Roman siege and destruction of the city. Thus it does not refer to Gentile believers living outside Judea such as the Colossian believers (3:12); Pauline converts (Tit 1:1); Gentile converts in Pontus, Galatia, Cappadocia, Asia and Bithynia (1 Pet 1:1); or God's people in general (Rev 17:14). They must be either Jewish people in general trapped inside Jerusalem or, in light of the context of Jesus speaking to his disciples (13:5-37), Jewish Christians trapped within the city who had not fled the city at the appearance of the sign of the abomination of desolation.[84]

MARK 13:21-23: THE WARNING OF FALSE MESSIANIC CLAIMANTS APPEARING SHORTLY BEFORE THE TEMPLE'S AND JERUSALEM'S DESTRUCTION

In 13:21-23 Mark concludes the unit begun in 13:5 with a warning against heeding those who claim that messiah(s) have appeared (13:21-22). The idea that the future coming of the Messiah would be a secret one conflicts with Christian teaching concerning "the blessed hope and the manifestation of the glory of our great God and Savior, Jesus Christ" (Tit 2:13). The Messiah's coming is associated with the resurrection of the dead (1 Thess 4:13-18) and "all the tribes of the earth will mourn, and they will see the 'Son of Man coming'" (Mt 24:30; cf. Lk 17:22-24), for he will come "with great power and glory" (Mk 13:26; 8:38). To what extent Mark's readers were aware of such teachings cannot be determined with certainty, but by the late sixties when Mark wrote his Gospel the future messianic hope of the return of Jesus Christ was a major belief and longing of the church as they prayed "*Marana tha*—Our Lord, come!" (1 Cor 16:22; Rev 22:20) and in the Lord's Prayer "Your kingdom come" (Mt 6:10; Lk 11:2). The existence of a common Aramaic

---

[82]Cf. Is 60:21-22; Sirach 36:10; *1 Enoch* 80:2; *2 Baruch* 20:1; 54:1; 83:1; 2 Esd 2:13; *Epistle of Barnabus* 4:3; *b. B. Mes.* 85b.

[83]In the New Testament this term is frequently used to describe Christians (Rom 8:33; Col 3:12; 2 Tim 2:10; Tit 1:1; 1 Pet 1:1; Rev 17:14). In the Old Testament it is used to describe the people of Israel or the believing remnant within Israel (e.g., Ps 105:6; Is 42:1; 43:20; 65:9, 15).

[84]France, *Mark*, p. 528.

prayer "*Marana tha*—Our Lord, come!" (1 Cor 16:22) in a Gentile Corinthian church in the early fifties indicates that this prayer was an integral part of the early Palestinian church that carried over to the Gentile churches. There is good reason to believe that it has its roots in the prayer Jesus taught his disciples (Mt 6:9-13/Lk 11:2-4) and Jesus' teachings about the coming of the Son of Man. The Lord might come suddenly and unexpectedly "like a thief in the night" (1 Thess 5:2; cf. Mt 24:42-44; Lk 12:39-40; 2 Pet 3:10; Rev 3:3; 16:15), but it would not be a secret coming! Thus the disciples are warned not to believe such false reports and rumors.

The warnings against false messianic and prophetic pretenders in 13:21-22 parallel the earlier warning found in 13:5-6 and form a chiasmus consisting of: A (13:5-6), B (13:7-20), A' (13:21-22). Here, however, in contrast to the earlier warning concerning the general appearance of such messianic pretenders, we have a specific warning concerning the appearance of such false messianic claimants associated with the destruction of Jerusalem. The appearance of such false claimants is well attested by Josephus in his *Jewish War*,[85] and the harm done by false prophets during the Jewish war is well documented by him (*J.W.* 6.285-88). Such false prophets may have falsely interpreted some of the early Jewish successes against the Romans as divine signs of salvation and deliverance.[86] These pretenders along with their prophecies would perform "signs and omens" that might even lead astray, "if possible, the elect." Mark does not discuss such questions as whether those who are truly elect can be led astray or whether God's plan could be altered (cf. Jesus' prayer that, "if it were possible, the hour might pass from him" in 14:35). The statement concerning the possibility of the elect being led astray might serve as a warning by Jesus to his disciples to "be all the more eager to confirm [their] call and election" (2 Pet 1:10), for even being one of the Twelve was no guarantee of salvation, as the apostasy of Judas Iscariot reveals. In the present context of Mark 13, however, the main issue is that these false messianic pretenders might deter the elect from fleeing Judea and Jerusalem to escape the coming Roman army.[87]

---

[85]For the appearance of false messiahs, see *J.W.* 2.433-48 (esp. 434-44); 4.503-44 (esp. 510); cf. also 2 Thess 2:8-12; 1 Jn 2:18. For the appearance of false prophets, see *J.W.* 6.285-300; cf. also Jer 6:13; 14:14; 23:32; Zech 13:2; Mt 7:15-20; 1 Jn 4:1; *Sibylline Oracles* 3.63-69.
[86]Marcus, *Mark 8–16*, p. 901.
[87]Lane, *Mark*, pp. 472-73.

The concluding verse of this section forms an *inclusio* with 13:5. The section begins with a "beware" (*blepete*, 13:5) and with Jesus repeating at its conclusion "be alert" or "beware" (*blepete*, 13:23).[88] It should be noted that the verb translated "beware" is emphatic as the *humeis* (*you*), which is unnecessary, indicates. In the context the "you" is directed at Peter, James, John and Andrew, and by implication to Jewish Christians in Judea and Jerusalem who on seeing the abomination of desolation should not allow themselves to be deceived by false prophets and messianic pretenders and seek safety in the fortress of Jerusalem. The "I have already told you everything" (13:23) also corresponds with the "tell us" in 13:4 and the "began to say" in 13:5, which all come from the same Greek verbal root (*legein/prolegein*). Finally, we should note the "everything" (*panta*) in 13:23, which corresponds with the "all these things" (*tauta panta*) in 13:4. With 13:23 we come to the end of Jesus' response and answer to the twofold question of the disciples (13:4) begun in 13:5. Jesus will next begin to teach something to the disciples concerning which they have not asked. The coming of the Son of Man will be a new subject not yet referred to but closely tied to the destruction of the temple and Jerusalem referred to in 13:1-23.

Summary

In summarizing the Markan message in 13:5-23, it is important once again to note that the material involves two settings in time. One involves the specific message of Jesus to his disciples answering their two-part question concerning the time of the destruction of the temple predicted by Jesus in 13:2 and the sign preceding it. The second involves what Mark is seeking to teach his readers by the Jesus traditions that he has collected and edited in 13:5-23. It is easy to intermix these two horizons of the text, and the result is confusion and lack of clarity in understanding either setting in time. Jesus' message for his disciples involves understanding that the temple and Jerusalem will be destroyed in their lifetime (cf. 13:30). Preceding this there will be false messianic pretenders and prophets, wars and

---

[88] It is unfortunate that most English translations use two different words in Mark 13:5 and 23 to translate the same Greek term *blepete*. The REB and the NKJV are exceptions. The former translates the term "be on your guard" in both instances, and the latter translates it "take heed!" in both.

rumors of wars, and earthly calamities, but they should not become unsettled by this. These things must take place and are part of the turmoil of a fallen world, but this does not mean the end of the temple is imminent. They do not indicate Jerusalem's impending destruction. As followers of Jesus, they will follow in his footsteps, and, as he already has told them (8:34-38), they will face trial before Jewish and Gentile authorities, and be hated by all segments of society, even their own families. Nevertheless despite and perhaps even because of all this the gospel will be proclaimed throughout the world (13:10), and faithful endurance, if need be to death, will result in eternal salvation. As to the destruction of the temple and Jerusalem, this will be preceded by the appearance of the abomination of desolation appearing in the temple. On seeing this, the disciples and other followers of Jesus living in Jerusalem and Judea should flee immediately for safety to the mountains. As for those living in Judea who seek protection and safety in the fortress of Jerusalem, they will experience such terrible and unimaginable tribulations that it is hard to think of anything that can compare to it.[89] Jesus concludes his teaching of the disciples concerning the destruction of Jerusalem with an exhortation and warning, "But [beware]; I have already told you everything."

What Mark is seeking to teach his readers by this material is not as easy to understand. It is not correct, however, to say, "For Mark himself, who probably writes his gospel far away from Judea for people living likewise far away from Judea . . . Jesus' instructions meet no practical need. Rather, they show his ability to predict the future in detail; they help form Mark's apology for the cross."[90] Christologically, the passage supports Jesus' claim that he is a prophet come from God, and, as Mark's readers compare what is happening in Judea, they recognize that Jesus' words are true. Consequently, they can trust in what he has taught them and promised them. The awareness of Jesus' role as prophet would also remind them that he is also the Christ, the true Messiah, the Son of Man, the Son of God. The truthfulness of his prophecies concerning what is happening in Jerusalem and Judea would also bring confidence of the truthfulness of his proph-

---

[89]Literally, "such tribulation as has not been from the beginning of the creation that God created until now, and never will be" (13:20).
[90]Gundry, *Mark*, p. 743.

ecies in the rest of this chapter and the Gospel of Mark as a whole. Thus they are encouraged to persevere in their tribulation (both present and future) in hope. As a result, even though Jesus has taught that his followers must bear a cross and endure to the end, they are his chosen elect and there awaits them, just like Jesus' disciples in Judea, a glorious kingdom. In addition, during the present time they are assured the presence of the Holy Spirit to guide and direct them.

5

The Coming of the Son of Man

Mark 13:24-27

TEXT AND INTRODUCTION

²⁴"But in those days, after that [tribulation, RSV],

the sun will be darkened,
and the moon will not give its light,
²⁵and the stars will be falling from heaven,
and the powers in the heavens will be shaken.

²⁶"Then they will see 'the Son of Man coming in clouds' with great power and glory. ²⁷Then he will send out the angels, and gather his elect from the four winds, from the ends of the earth to the ends of heaven."

The material in this section consists of an introduction separating this material from the preceding (13:24a), a series of cosmic signs indicating a theophany (13:24b-25), and the theophany itself involving the coming of the Son of Man and his gathering of the elect from throughout the world (13:26-27). The key interpretative issues in this passage involve the temporal relationship of this material with the preceding, how to interpret the cosmic imagery found in 13:24b-25, and whether the interpretation of the coming of the Son of Man and the gathering of the elect from the ends of the earth in 13:26-27 involves a literal, future coming of Jesus Christ that brings history as we know it to an end, or whether it is to be interpreted metaphorically as somehow having taken place in the destruction of the temple and Jerusalem in A.D. 70.

MARK 13:24A: "BUT IN THOSE DAYS, AFTER THAT TRIBULATION"

With the temporal introduction "but . . . after that [tribulation]," Mark indicates to his readers that he is beginning a new section and topic. He does so by the adversative "but" (*alla*) and the temporal designation "after that [tribulation]." Some argue that "but" acts as a strong adversative introducing an entirely new subject.[1] However, whereas "but" (*alla*) is used forty-five times in Mark, it is never used to indicate the beginning of an altogether new section.[2] On the other hand, "but" along with "after that [tribulation]" and the change in subject matter does indicate that we are dealing with a new theme taking place after the destruction of the temple and Jerusalem described in 13:15-23.[3] One should not assume that the tribulation referred to is "the great tribulation" (RSV) of Revelation 7:14. The expression "the great tribulation" is found only this one time in the New Testament, whereas the term *tribulation* is used forty-five times and the adjective *great* is used only twice with respect to it. The second instance where *great* is associated with the term *tribulation* (RSV) is Matthew 24:21, but here it is used to describe the intensity of the tribulation associated with the destruction of Jerusalem and does not designate "the" great tribulation.[4] These two temporal designations ("in those days," "after that [tribulation]") along with the *inclusio* in 13:23 (see pp. 67, 72, 100 above), indicate that 13:5-23 is a unity, and that a new subject is being introduced at this point that possesses the greatest relevance in this chapter for Mark's Gentile readers.[5]

Still another indicator that we are involved with something new in 13:24-27 is the clear change in the audience being addressed. It is clear that the audience envisioned in 13:5-23 is the disciples. This is evident by the "you" (always plural except in the verb "look" [*ide*], 13:21) found in 13:5

---

[1] So William L. Lane, *The Gospel According to Mark*, NICNT (Grand Rapids: Eerdmans, 1974), p. 483n87; Joachim Gnilka, *Das Evangelium nach Markus (Mk 8,27–16,20)*, EKKNT 2/2 (Zurich: Benzinger, 1979), p. 200; Rudolf Pesch, *Das Markusevangelium*, part 2: *Kommentur zu 8,27–16,20*, 2nd ed., HTKNT (Freiburg: Herder, 1981), p. 302; Ben Witherington III, *The Gospel of Mark: A Socio-Rhetorical Commentary* (Grand Rapids: Eerdmans, 2001), p. 347.

[2] Timothy C. Gray, *The Temple in the Gospel of Mark: A Study in Its Narrative Role* (Grand Rapids: Baker, 2010), pp. 137-39. This argues against the view of Camille Focant, *The Gospel According to Mark: A Commentary*, trans. L. R. Keylock (Eugene, OR: Pickwick, 2012), p. 543, that the *alla* ("but") is to be interpreted as standing in contrast to the *de* ("but") of 13:23 and starting a new subject.

[3] Compare Adela Y. Collins, "The Apocalyptic Rhetoric of Mark 13 in Historical Context," *Biblical Research* 41 (1996): 29, who argues that "the temporal indicator ['but ... after that tribulation'] and the shift in subject matter in vs 24a mark the beginning of a new unit."

[4] Eckhard Schnabel, *40 Questions About the End Times* (Grand Rapids: Kregel, 2011), p. 79.

[5] A. M. Ambrozic, *The Hidden Kingdom: A Redaction-Critical Study of the References to the Kingdom of God in Mark's Gospel*, CBQMS 2 (Washington, DC: Catholic Biblical Association of America), p. 228-29; Collins, "Apocalyptic Rhetoric," pp. 29-30.

(2x), 7 (2x), 9 (5x), 11 (6x), 13, 14, 18, 21 (4x) and 23 (3x).[6] It is clear from 13:3-4 that the referent of "you" is the disciples, represented by Peter, James, John and Andrew. On the other hand, the disciples are not addressed in 13:24-27, and the second person pronoun (singular or plural) and second person verbs (singular or plural) are nowhere found. The material is not addressed to the "when you see" audience in 13:14 but rather to a nondescript "they will see" audience in 13:26. In the following parable of the fig tree (13:28-31) the audience addressed is once again the disciples (note the "you" in 13:28 [2x], 29 [3x], 30, who are part of "this generation" in 13:30). In 13:32-37 the disciples are again referred to (note the "you" in the exhortations found in 13:33 [3x], 35 [2x], 36, 37 [2x]), because no one knows the exact time of the coming of the Son of Man (13:32). Thus the exhortations are relevant to them as well.

There is, however, a connection between the coming of the Son of Man in 13:24-27 and the destruction of the temple referred in 13:2, 4, 5-23. The expression "in those days" appears to tie these two events together temporally in some manner.[7] Some scholars also argue that there is more than just a temporal tie between two different events. They argue that these are essentially two different descriptions, one literal (13:5-23) and the other metaphorical (13:24-27), of the same event—the destruction of the temple and Jerusalem and its significance in salvation history. It has been argued that "in those days" is a technical term describing a theophany or divine intervention into history involving judgment or restoration. Support for this can be found in numerous passages: Jeremiah 3:16, 18; 5:18; 31:29; 33:15-16; 50:4; Joel 2:29; 3:1; Zechariah 8:23; and so on. But the expression can also be used to refer to a particular period of time that has no specific theophanic significance. It is probably used in this way in Mark 13:17 (cf. also 13:19-20) with respect to the time of Jerusalem's forthcoming destruction and the terrible tribulation associated with it. It is clear, however, that in the great majority of instances in the Gospels "in those days" is not used in a technical sense referring to a future theophany but in a historical

---

[6]These numbers come from the Greek text and involve pronouns and second-person verbal forms.
[7]Gray, *Temple in the Gospel of Mark*, pp. 138-39; but compare Focant (*Mark*, p. 543), who argues that the expression "in those days" is "not a precise temporal indication; it rather maintains a fuzziness from the chronological viewpoint."

sense looking back to a past event (e.g., Mk 1:9; 4:35 [singular]; 8:1; Mt 3:1; Lk 2:1; 4:2; 5:35; 9:36). In 13:24 (cf. also 13:32) it is used in the theophanic sense as the references to the cosmic signs and the coming of the Lord (*kyrios*) in 13:35 suggest.

The existence of a temporal connection between 13:14-23 and 13:24-27 seems clear. *But* it is also clear that these two events are separated in time, for the coming of the Son of Man occurs "after" the tribulation associated with the destruction of the temple and Jerusalem described in 13:5-23. "But . . . after that [tribulation]" indicates that 13:24-27 is not simply a repetition of the destruction of Jerusalem described in 13:5-23 using metaphorical, cosmic language! It involves a different event! Yet the coming of the Son of Man will nevertheless occur "in those days." Matthew in his parallel passage ties the coming even more closely in time by stating, "Immediately after the tribulation of those days" (24:29 RSV). One attempted explanation of the temporal gap between the destruction of Jerusalem in A.D. 70 and the "not yet" of the coming of the Son of Man involves the idea of having a "prophetic perspective" in interpreting this passage. This involves viewing prophetic passages of Scripture as a landscape painting,[8] "which marks distinctly the houses, paths, and bridges in the foreground, but brings together, into a narrow space, the distant valleys and mountains, though they are really far apart."[9] The present writer has experienced something like this while watching a baseball game on television. At one point the center-field television camera zeroed in on the pitcher's mound and the discussion taking place there. It appeared that the center-fielder, second baseman, runner on second base, pitcher, catcher, manager, batter and umpire were all together discussing something at the mound. The order in which they were standing was relatively clear, but the distance between them was not.[10] Similarly, in our passage, the existence of a temporal gap between the destruction of Jerusalem and the coming of

---

[8]Cf. George R. Beasley-Murray, *Jesus and the Last Days: The Interpretation of the Olivet Discourse* (Peabody, MA: Hendrickson, 1993), pp. 127-28, who suggests that Johann Albrecht Bengel was the first to suggest this method of interpretation.
[9]Ibid., p. 128.
[10]William Hendriksen, *Exposition of the Gospel According to Mark*, NTC (Grand Rapids: Baker, 1975), p. 526, suggests that Jesus portrays the future as he sees it. Yet the closer one comes to the first peak (the destruction of the temple and Jerusalem), the clearer one sees the distance between this and the next peak (the parousia).

the Son of Man is clear (*"But ... after that [tribulation]"*), but the length of that gap is uncertain ("in those days").[11] There is nothing wrong in seeking to harmonize biblical passages in such a manner.[12] What is wrong is when shoddy and incorrect exegesis of the text(s) is used to support such a harmonization.

Among the various attempts to make sense of the data is one that assumes that the tribulation referred to in 13:5-23 refers to a future "great" tribulation preceding the coming of the Son of Man. Another assumes that 13:5-23 refers to the destruction of Jerusalem in A.D. 70 and that the coming of the Son of Man refers to something connected to this in both time and meaning. In the summary of this section below we will discuss this perspective and also the fact that Matthew, who wrote his Gospel some fifteen years after the destruction of Jerusalem, could write that "*Immediately* after the [tribulation] of those days" the Son of Man would appear (24:29-30).

Mark 13:24b-25: The Appearance of Theophanic Signs

In seeking to understand this passage the question arises as to whether the language found in these verses should be understood "literally" or "figuratively."[13] For the present-day reader who is unfamiliar with various Old Testament genres such as poetry, proverbs, prophecy, apocalyptic, psalms, hyperbole and so on, this is difficult. The imagery of 13:24b-25, however, is found frequently in the Old Testament, and Jesus and his hearers, as well as the Gospel writers and their readers, were familiar with such passages as the following:

---

[11]For another attempt to reconcile such "time problems," see G. B. Caird, *The Language and Imagery of the Bible* (Philadelphia: Westminister, 1980), pp. 256-67.

[12]The present writer once experienced a young doctoral student seeking to harmonize two apparently contradictory biblical passages and heard the professor dismiss his explanation by simply saying, "Das is nur Harmonizerung!" No reasons were presented as to why the explanation was flawed or incorrect. It was enough to say "That is simply a harmonization" to dismiss the argument. Suggested harmonizations or explanations of biblical passages are neither right nor wrong because they are harmonizations. The rightness or wrongness of such attempts depends on the rightness or wrongness of the reasoning of such explanations!

[13]The distinction here is overly simplistic, but it avoids the more cumbersome use of such qualifying terms as "primarily literal" and "primarily figurative" or "primarily literal" or "primarily symbolic," and so on. See Dale C. Allison Jr., "Jesus & the Victory of Apocalyptic," in *Jesus & the Restoration of Israel: A Critical Assessment of N. T. Wright's Jesus and the Victory of God*, ed. Carey C. Newman (Downers Grove, IL: InterVarsity Press, 1999), pp. 130-34.

Isaiah 13:9-11

See, the day of the LORD comes,
cruel, with wrath and fierce anger,
to make the earth a desolation,
and to destroy its sinners from it.
For the stars of the heavens and their constellations
will not give their light;
the sun will be dark at its rising,
and the moon will not shed its light.
I will punish the world for its evil,
and the wicked for their iniquity;
I will put an end to the pride of the arrogant,
and lay low the insolence of the tyrants. (italics added)

Although we find cosmic imagery in 13:10 ("for the stars . . . light"), the judgment referred to is one that was coming on the Babylonian Empire (13:1, 19) by their enemies, the Medes (13:17-18). This (Is 13:1-22) was fulfilled in 539 B.C. Clearly the cosmic imagery that describes the end of the Babylonian Empire was understood by later readers of Isaiah as figurative language describing the judgment that the God of Israel ("the LORD," 13:9) who rules the heavens had brought on Babylon. The cosmic signs did not "literally" take place, but the divine judgment of God to which these signs referred was "literally" fulfilled.

Jeremiah 4:23-26

I looked on the earth, and lo, it was waste and void;
and to the heavens, and they had no light.
I looked on the mountains, and lo, they were quaking,
and all the hills moved to and fro.
I looked, and lo, there was no one at all,
and all the birds of the air had fled.
I looked, and lo, the fruitful land was a desert,
and all its cities were laid in ruins,
before the LORD, *before his fierce anger.* (italics added)

Here again we find cosmic language (4:23) along with unusual geographical and topological events that describe the destruction of Jerusalem (4:5, 11, 14,

16, 31; 5:1, 11, 20; 6:1-2, 6-9, 23; 15:5) by the Babylonians (4:6-7; 5:15; 6:1, 22) in 587 B.C. (4:1–6:30). As in the preceding example in Isaiah 13:9-11, whereas the Medes and Babylonians are the instruments of judgment, the ultimate cause is God. This is indicated by the cosmic terminology used in the passage, as well as direct statements to this effect.[14]

Ezekiel 32:7-8

When I blot you out, I will cover the heavens,
and make their stars dark;
I will cover the sun with a cloud,
and the moon shall not give its light.
⁸All the shining lights of the heavens I will darken above you,
and put darkness on your land,
says the Lord God. (italics added)

In this instance the cosmic terminology describes the judgment coming on Hophra, Pharaoh of Egypt, and his army in 585 B.C. (32:1) by the Babylonians under Nebuchadnezzar (29:17-20; 30:10-26; 32:10-11). Again this imagery is used metaphorically to indicate that God is bringing judgment on Egypt. What is about to happen to the Pharaoh of Egypt is not simply an accidental event of history but an earth-shattering event over which God ruled.

Amos 8:9-10

On that day, says the Lord God,
  I will make the sun go down at noon,
  and darken the earth in broad daylight.
I will turn your feasts into mourning,
  and all your songs into lamentation;
I will bring sackcloth on all loins,
  and baldness on every head;
I will make it like the mourning for an only son,
  and the end of it like a bitter day. (italics added)

---

[14]Cf. Is 13:3 ("I myself have commanded"); Is 13:11 ("I will punish"); Is 13:12 ("I will make mortals more rare"); Is 13:13 ("I will make the heavens tremble"); Jer 4:12b ("Now it is I who speak in judgment against them"); Jer 5:19 ("And when your people say, 'Why has the Lord our God done all these things to us?'"); Jer 6:19 ("Hear, O earth; I am going to bring disaster on this people").

In this earlier prophecy by Amos, the prophet pronounces God's coming judgment on the northern kingdom of Israel. Due to its oppression and neglect of the poor described in the preceding verses (8:4-6), God has sworn that judgment will inevitably come on the nation of Israel (8:7-8). This judgment came in 722 B.C. at the hands of the Assyrians when they destroyed the capital city, Samaria and its temple, and led the leading citizens into exile. This resulted in these ten tribes becoming "the lost tribes of Israel."

Acts 2:16-21

No, this is what was spoken through the prophet Joel:

"In the last days it will be, God declares,
that I will pour out my Spirit on all flesh,
 and your sons and your daughters shall prophesy,
and your young men shall see visions,
 and your old men shall dream dreams.
Even upon my slaves, both men and women,
 in those days I will pour out my Spirit;
  and they shall prophesy.
And I will show portents in the heaven above
 and signs on the earth below,
  blood, and fire, and smoky mist.
The sun shall be turned to darkness
 and the moon to blood,
  before the coming of the Lord's great and glorious day.
Then everyone who calls on the name of the Lord shall be saved." (italics added)

This passage is an excellent example of how Peter (and Luke) understood various cosmic descriptions found in Old Testament prophesies as being metaphorical in nature. In Acts 2:14-16 Peter explains to the "Men of Judah and all who live in Jerusalem" (2:14) that the speaking in foreign languages (Acts 2:6-11) was evidence that the awaited coming of the Spirit, prophesied by Joel (Joel 2:28-32), was taking place. Although some argue that the cosmic signs referred to in 2:19-20 indicate a future event,[15] Peter's words ("No, this

---

[15]So John B. Polhill, *Acts*, NAC (Nashville: Broadman, 1992), pp. 108-10; Darrell L. Bock, *Acts*, BECNT (Grand Rapids: Baker Academic, 2007), pp. 115-17.

[the events of 2:5-13] is what was spoken through the prophet Joel") are best understood as referring to the present fulfillment of the whole quotation of Joel 2:28-32 (3:1-5 in the Hebrew Bible and LXX), not just to what is referred to in Acts 2:17-18, 21 but also Acts 2:19-20. This is clearly how Luke understood the prophecy. He reveals this same understanding of cosmic and topological imagery in Luke 3:4-6 when he refers to the coming of John the Baptist in his quotation of Isaiah 40:3-5:

As it is written in the book of the words of the prophet Isaiah,

"The voice of one crying out in the wilderness:
'Prepare the way of the Lord,
    make his paths straight.
Every valley shall be filled,
    and every mountain and hill shall be made low,
and the crooked shall be made straight,
    and the rough ways made smooth;
and all flesh shall see the salvation of God.'" (italics added)[16]

The poetic references to these topographical changes in the prophecy of Isaiah are not understood literally by Luke as involving massive geographical changes in the structural configuration of the planet. Rather they are understood by him as hyperbolic and metaphorical portrayals as to what the coming of John the Baptist indicated. The kingdom of God had come! A theophanic event was taking place. The proud and arrogant were being humbled and the humble were being exalted (Lk 1:52; 14:11; 18:14). The longed-for hope and desire of Israel had arrived.[17]

It is evident from the above that the Old Testament prophets were familiar with and frequently used cosmic terminology to express a theophany in which God would act in history for judgment and/or blessing. The writers did not intend that this language should be interpreted "literalistically," for

---

[16]For similar figurative language used by Old Testament writers compare Judg 5:4-5 (note that no earthquakes and mountains shaking are referred to in the narrative account describing this event in Judg 4); Ps 18:7-9; 77:18; 82:5; Amos 9:5; Mic 1:4; Nahum 1:5; Hab 3:6.

[17]Note how the term *low* (*tapeinōthēsetai*) in 3:5 is used in 14:11 where God is referred to as exalting those who "humble" themselves. Whereas the one exalting himself will be "humbled" (*tapeinōthēsetai*), the one humbling himself (*tapeinōn*) will be exalted. The same terminology is used again in 18:14b.

the fulfillment of these prophecies was not associated with such cosmic phenomena. This was evident to those who read such accounts during the intertestamental and New Testament times. Thus Jesus and Mark were very familiar with the use of such cosmic language in prophecy. Another important fact that should be noted is that the passages quoted above appear in poetic form in most English translations.[18] Thus these accounts should be read not as examples of historical narrative, but rather as poetic expressions of God's actions in history.

Whereas cosmic imagery in prophecy refers to a coming theophanic event in which God would act in history, what exactly that theophany would involve is not indicated by the imagery itself. The content of the theophany is clarified by the context in which it is found. In the passages quoted above the content of the theophany is revealed by the prophets' declarations that the Babylonian Empire will be destroyed by the Medes (Is 13:9-11), Jerusalem will be destroyed by Babylon (Jer 4:23-27), Pharaoh Hophra of Egypt and his army will be destroyed by Nebuchadnezzar (Ezek 32:7-8), Israel will cease to exist by the Assyrian destruction of the city of Samaria in 722 B.C. and the exile of its leading citizens (Amos 8:9-10), and the gift of the Spirit had come at Pentecost and henceforth will be given to all who "call on the name of the Lord" (Acts 2:16-21). In Mark 13 the content of the coming theophany is indicated by the "[And] then" (*kai tote*) of 13:26. The cosmic phenomena in these verses are not related to the "sign" that the disciples asked for in 13:4.[19] That sign has already been given in 13:14 and involves the appearance of the abomination of desolation preceding the destruction of the temple and Jerusalem and calling for immediate flight. The cosmic phenomena in 13:24b-25 are not the sign indicating that the destruction of the temple and Jerusalem are imminent, for these phenomena will occur "after" these events. Neither are they preliminary signs after that destruction announcing the coming of the Son of Man. They are rather accompaniments of his coming.[20]

---

[18]This is true in the ESV, NAB, NJB, NLB, NRSV (which does not record Joel 2:30-32 as poetry) and REB (which does not record Ezekiel 32:7-8 or Acts 2:17-21 as poetry).
[19]Contra M. Eugene Boring, *Mark*, NTL (Louisville: Westminster John Knox, 2006), p. 372.
[20]Beasley-Murray, *Jesus and the Last Days*, pp. 189, 307.

Mark 13:26-27: The Coming of the Son of Man

A number of issues present themselves in seeking to understand the meaning of these verses. One involves the referent of the "'Son of Man coming in clouds' with great power and glory." The traditional interpretation of 13:26 maintains that this refers to a future event in which the Son of Man will return from heaven to judge the living and the dead and bring an end to the space-time universe in which we now live. Some scholars, however, argue that, since no specific mention is made in 13:26-27 of the Son of Man coming to judge the world, the parousia is to be interpreted as uniquely and only positive in nature.[21] Yet 13:26-27 must be interpreted in light of 8:38 where Jesus states, "Those who are ashamed of me and of my words in this adulterous and sinful generation, of them the Son of Man will also be ashamed when he comes in the glory of his Father with the holy angels." The one who is ashamed of Jesus and his teachings, the Son of Man will be ashamed of when he comes in glory. Such an event clearly envisions a judgment in which believers are separated from nonbelievers who forfeit their soul (8:36). Whereas "the prime purpose of the theophanic parousia is for the deliverance of the people of God . . . that cannot be imagined without the exercise of judgment."[22] The various passages in the New Testament which associate the parousia of Jesus the Son of Man with judgment[23] also suggest that the readers of Mark were familiar with such teachings and would have assumed that the coming of the Son of Man in 13:24-27 would involve judgment. The fact that most theophanies in the Bible involve judgment even more so than salvation also strongly argues that Mark assumed his readers would recognize that the parousia involved both blessing for God's people and judgment for those who reject God's offer of salvation.

Allowing for various degrees of figurative language, the traditional view presented above assumes a literal, visual return of Jesus of Nazareth as the Son of Man that brings an end to history as we know it. Some who hold this

---

[21]Cf. Focant, *Mark*, pp. 544-45, who states, "This is typical of the spirit of Mark's gospel, in which no text treating the Son of Man includes a threatening person." Focant, however, is clearly ignoring Mark 8:38.

[22]Beasley-Murray, *Jesus and the Last Days*, p. 430.

[23]Cf. Mt 13:36-43; 16:27; 19:28; 24:36-44, 45-51; 25:1-13, 14-30, 31-46; Lk 12:8-9; Jn 5:25-29; Acts 17:31; 1 Cor 4:5; 2 Thess 1:5-10; 2:8-10; 2 Tim 4:1; 2 Pet 3:10; Jude 14-15; Rev 19:1-21. It should, of course, not be assumed that the readers of Mark were familiar with all these teachings. But even more should it not be assumed that they were ignorant of all such teachings!

view would add an earthly, millennial reign by the Son of Man somewhere before the final judgment. Those who reject a more literal interpretation of Mark 13:26-27, in which the Son of Man brings judgment and the end of the world, have suggested a number of different interpretations. One is that the language of 13:26-27 is essentially a figurative critique of the social and political makeup of the present world order with various proposed changes. Another is that these verses metaphorically predict major, drastic events coming on Israel in order to change her ways so as to avoid disaster in this present time and space world. Another proposes that we recognize the mythical nature of the language of these verses and demythologize them, in order to understand their underlying existential meaning, and experience escape from the bondage of the flesh and law in order to enjoy the freedom of the Spirit.[24] For our purposes such interpretations are not relevant with respect to our goal of understanding the consciously intended meaning of Mark 13, whether of the Jesus of history or the Evangelist Mark.

A more recent interpretation that has gained some support suggests the use of end-of-the-world language in Mark 13:24-27 as the only metaphors adequate to express the significance of what was about to happen to Israel, Jerusalem and her temple and the fulfillment of her "return from exile" as promised by the prophets.[25] This view argues that Mark 13:5-23 refers to the literal destruction of the temple that took place in A.D. 70. The cosmic language of 13:24b-25 indicates that this destruction is a theophanic event in which God brings judgment on unbelieving Israel through the instrumentality of Rome. Similarly, the cosmic imagery of the coming of the Son of Man in 13:26-27 does not refer to some yet unfulfilled event in the future in which the Son of Man will come from heaven to judge the world and gather the elect from throughout the world. This cosmic imagery, like that in 13:24b-25, is to be interpreted figuratively not as referring to a future event but to one that would be contemporaneous with the destruction of the temple and Jerusalem and its positive corollary—Jesus' vindication by the fulfillment of his prophecy and the establishment of an international people of God. Mark 13:26-27 is to be understood as part of the answer to

---

[24]See the discussion in N. T. Wright, *Jesus and the Victory of God* (Minneapolis: Fortress, 1996), pp. 208-14.
[25]Ibid., pp. 320-68.

the "when" of Jerusalem's destruction that the disciples asked about in 13:4. "When Jerusalem is destroyed, and Jesus' people escape from the ruin just in time, *that will be* YHWH becoming king, bringing about the liberation of his true covenant people, the true return from exile, the beginning of the new world order."[26]

The above interpretation offers several solutions for some of the difficulties associated with Mark 13:24-27. For one it resolves the temporal problem of "in those days." Whereas many interpreters like to separate temporally the destruction of the temple described in 13:5-23 and the events of 13:24-27 interpreted as a not-yet parousia of the Son of Man, this interpretation eliminates any temporal problem that "in those days" raises by interpreting the coming of the Son of Man figuratively as the liberation of "true Israel" and the beginning of a new age resulting from the destruction of the temple in A.D. 70. Thus the statement of Jesus in 13:30 that "this generation will not pass away until all these things have taken place" is resolved, for "all these things" would soon take place in the imminent destruction of Jerusalem. This interpretation is also correct in arguing that 13:5-23 is about the destruction of Jerusalem in A.D. 70, so future events such as the coming of a great tribulation, the coming of the antichrist, the parousia and the end of the world should not be read into it.

There are numerous problems, however, with the above interpretation of Mark 13:24-27 that make it less convincing than the traditional one. One problem involves the issue of determining when we are dealing with something meant to be interpreted figuratively and when it is meant to be interpreted literally. In the Old Testament examples given above, the cosmic language used should be interpreted figuratively; the material following, however, is best interpreted in a more literal manner: Isaiah 13:10 figuratively, but Isaiah 13:11 more literally; Jeremiah 4:23-24 figuratively, but Jeremiah 4:25-26 more literally; Ezekiel 32:7-8 figuratively, but Ezekiel 32:9-10 more literally; Amos 8:9 figuratively, but Amos 8:10-11 more literally; and Acts 2:19-20 figuratively, but Acts 2:18, 21 more literally. In a similar way the figu-

---

[26]Ibid., p. 364. Cf. also p. 340: "The destruction coming on YHWH's chosen city would be like that which fell on Babylon. The exile was coming to an end at last." Note, however, that this view assumes that whereas the destruction of Jerusalem by Babylon in 587 B.C. led to the exile of Israel, the destruction of Jerusalem by Rome in A.D. 70 supposedly leads to the very opposite—the return from exile!

rative, cosmic language of Mark 13:24-25 is followed by the description of a more literal event—the "seeing" of the Son of Man coming from heaven.

The "coming of the Son of Man" is not simply "good first-century metaphorical language for two things: the defeat of the enemies of the true people of God, and the vindication of the true people themselves."[27] This is evident because this definition cannot be substituted for the "coming of the Son of Man" in such passages as Mark 8:38; 14:62; Acts 1:11; 1 Corinthians 15:23; 1 Thessalonians 4:15; 2 Thessalonians 2:1; Titus 2:13; and 2 Peter 3:4. Such a substitution would make no sense. Mark 8:38 is especially important in this regard. This earlier reference to the Son of Man coming in glory and judgment with the holy angels is "determinative . . . [and] establishes the way in which the others should be read."[28] When we consider the context in which Mark's readers would have heard this passage, it is evident they would have assumed that the title "Son of Man" referred to the risen Jesus of Nazareth coming from heaven in great glory. In Acts 1:9 Jesus is described as ascending into heaven and that "a cloud took him out of their [the disciples'] sight," and in 1:11 the angel tells the disciples that "this Jesus, who has been taken up from you into heaven, will come in *the same way as you saw him go into heaven*" (italics added). In 1 Thessalonians 4:15-17 Paul states concerning the coming (*parousian*) of the Lord that "the Lord himself . . . will descend from heaven . . . [and] we who are alive . . . will be caught up in the clouds together with them to meet the Lord in the air." The "coming of the Lord" is also referred to in 2 Thessalonians 2:1 ("As to the coming [*parousias*] of our Lord Jesus Christ and our being gathered together to him"), 1 Corinthians 15:23 ("Christ . . . at his coming [*parousia*]") and Titus 2:13 (which refers to our waiting "for the blessed hope and the manifestation of the glory of our great God and Savior, Jesus Christ"). Paul writes to the Corinthians and ends his first letter with the Aramaic prayer *Marana tha*. Most English translations now translate the prayer "Our Lord, come!" This is unfortunate in that it hides the fact that Paul writes this prayer to his Greek readers in Corinth in a language the

---

[27]Ibid., p. 362. Cf. Scot McKnight, *A New Vision for Israel: The Teachings of Jesus in National Context* (Grand Rapids: Eerdmans, 1999), p. 135, who writes, "The disciples will escape persecution because God will act to vindicate Jesus, as Son of Man, by permitting Rome to wreak God's vengeance on a disobedient people."

[28]Edward Adams, "The Coming of the Son of Man in Mark's Gospel," *Tyndale Bulletin* 56, no. 2 (2005): 60.

Corinthians did not know—Aramaic! Yet this prayerful yearning was so much a fundamental element in the worship of the early Christian community that it was repeated and memorized even by those who knew no Aramaic. Later the Greek form of this prayer became a part of the worship of the early church (cf. Rev 22:20). Second Peter 3:4, 10, 12 likewise speaks of the coming of the Lord (cf. also Jn 21:22-23; 1 Thess 5:2, 4).

Perhaps the most striking parallel to Mark 13:26-27 is found in 1 Thessalonians 4:16-17. Compare them:

> Then they will see the "Son of Man coming in clouds" with great power and glory. Then he will send out the angels, and gather his elect from the four winds, from the ends of the earth to the ends of heaven. (Mark 13:26-27)

> For the Lord himself, with a cry of command, with the archangel's call and with the sound of God's trumpet, will descend from heaven, and the dead in Christ will rise first. Then we who are alive, who are left, will be caught up in the clouds together with them to meet the Lord in the air; and so we will be with the Lord forever. (1 Thess 4:16-17)

The remarkable similarity between these two passages should be noted. "These passages look very much like oral variants of a tradition that may well go back to Jesus."[29] It should also be noted that 1 Thessalonians 4:16-17 predates the written form of this tradition in Mark 13:26-27 by fifteen to twenty years and that in the tradition of the Lord's return in 1 Thessalonians Paul does not associate the parousia in any way with the destruction of Jerusalem in A.D. 70.

We also find the language of Mark 13:26-27 in other end-time statements of Jesus. In Matthew 13:40-42 Jesus refers to "the end of the age," the final judgment and "the furnace of fire," and we find the terms "Son of Man," "will send" and "angels" that appear in Mark 13:26-27. In Matthew 16:27-28 (cf. Mk 8:38; Lk 9:26) Jesus speaks of the final judgment of everyone as individuals at his coming, and we find the terms "Son of Man," "to come," "angels" and "glory," as in Mark 13:26-27. In Matthew 25:31 Jesus refers to the Son of Man coming in judgment resulting in eternal punishment or eternal life (25:46), and we again find the terms "Son of Man," "comes," "glory" and "angels" as

---

[29] Adela Y. Collins and John J. Collins, *King and Messiah as Son of God: Divine, Human, and Angelic Messianic Figures in Biblical and Related Literature* (Grand Rapids: Eerdmans, 2008), p. 172.

in Mark 13:26-27. Finally, in Mark 14:62 (cf. Mt 26:64) Jesus refers to his enthronement (cf. Acts 2:33; 5:31; Ps 110:1) as the "Son of Man," his subsequent "coming," and "clouds" as in Mark 13:26-27.

From all this it is evident that the dominating milieu from which Mark and the other New Testament writers understood the reference to Jesus coming in the clouds of heaven with great glory was not a hypothetical interpretation of what the author of Daniel 7:13 meant,[30] but rather the Jesus traditions that they possessed and were taught by the "eyewitnesses and servants of the word" (Lk 1:2) and the other apostolic teachings they possessed, whether in oral or written form. We cannot assume that the author of Mark (as well as his readers) knew all these traditions concerning the parousia of Jesus given above, but he clearly knew those found in his Gospel, and he undoubtedly knew more than he wrote (cf. John 21:25). Concerning his understanding of 13:26-27, it appears reasonable therefore to conclude, "Since Mark's other references to the coming of the son of man refer to a future appearance that will be seen by people on earth (8:38; 14:62), the traditional interpretation seems justified."[31]

Summary

Mark 13:24-27 begins the second part of Mark 13. The first part focuses on Jesus' statement concerning the destruction of the temple and Jerusalem in 13:2 in response to the disciples' statement concerning the magnificence of the temple. Jesus, impressed less by the architectural and aesthetical beauty of the temple than by its spiritual and moral poverty, points to the divine judgment soon to fall upon it.[32] The response of Jesus to the two-part question in 13:4 is marked off by an introductory "Then Jesus began to say to them" (13:5) and a concluding "I have already told you everything" (13:23). These two statements serve as bookends forming an *inclusio* so that 13:5-23 forms a unit in which Jesus answers the two-part question of the disciples in 13:4.

This twofold division of Mark 13 is made even clearer by the opening statement in 13:24-27: "But in those days, after that [tribulation, RSV]."

---

[30]Contra R. T. France, *The Gospel of Mark*, NIGTC (Grand Rapids: Eerdmans, 2002), p. 503.
[31]Mary Ann Beavis, *Mark*, Paideia (Grand Rapids: Baker Academic, 2011), p. 200.
[32]Compare how Paul also was less impressed by the architectural beauty of the Parthenon and the Acropolis of Athens than by its idolatry (Acts 17:16, 19-31).

Whereas 13:1-23 deals with the destruction of the temple and the tribulation associated with it (cf. 13:19, "suffering, such as has not been from the beginning of the creation that God created until now, no, and never will be"), 13:24-27 deals with a period *after* that suffering and tribulation. Although there is a temporal connection between 13:24-27 and what has preceded ("in those days"), there is an even stronger disconnect between them ("But . . . after that tribulation [suffering]"—that is, the one referred to in 13:19).

Regardless of exactly what Mark wanted his readers to understand by "in those days" (13:24a), he clearly wanted them to understand that 13:24b-27 occurs *after* the destruction of the temple and Jerusalem described in 13:5-23! The cosmic theophany of 13:24b-25 refers to something that God was going to do, and it comes downward from heaven to earth, not upward from earth to heaven. The existence of numerous references in the New Testament to Jesus descending from heaven to earth to bring blessing on his church and judgment on his enemies forms the milieu by which the hearers of Jesus and the readers of Mark would have interpreted this cosmic language. Their daily prayers "thy kingdom come" and *Marana tha* predisposed them to interpret the cosmic language of 13:24b-25 as seeking the fulfillment of this through "the blessed hope and the manifestation of the glory of [their] God and Savior, Jesus Christ" (Tit 2:13). It would not have been understood as being fulfilled in God bringing judgment on unbelieving Israel through the instrumentality of the Roman Empire. Nor would they have understood the gathering of the elect by the Son of Man from the four corners of the earth as referring to the escape of the followers of Jesus from Jerusalem in A.D. 70 and their being scattered even further throughout the world. The Old Testament prophecies to which Mark 13:27 alludes speak of the gathering from Assyria, Egypt, Pathros, Ethiopia, Elam, Shinar, Hamath, the coastlands of the sea, the Euphrates, the land of the north and from all directions—north, south, east and west—toward the exiles' homeland, the holy mountain of Jerusalem, Zion.[33] The direction should be noted. *It is not from Jerusalem outward to the ends of the earth but inward from the ends of the earth to Jerusalem!*

Mark 13:24-27 is best understood as a theophanic act of God in which the Son of Man comes from heaven and sends his angels to gather his elect from

---

[33]See Is 11:11-12; 27:12-13; 35:1-10; 43:5-13; 49:22; 60:1-9; 66:20; Jer 23:7-8; 31:10-14; Ezek 39:25-29; Zech 10:6-12; cf. also Tob 13:13; Bar 5:5-9; *Psalms of Solomon* 11:1-9.

the four winds or corners of the earth. (Note it is not God's elect but "his" [the Son of Man's] elect! The Christology contained in the use of the pronoun *his* is a lofty one indeed!) This section concerning the Son of Man will be completed in 13:32-37 by a parable concerning the unknowable nature of the time of the Son of Man's coming. No one, not even the angels in heaven nor the Son knows, but only God himself. Consequently, Jesus' hearers and Mark's readers will be exhorted to be vigilant and alert.

The biggest problem encountered in 13:24-27 involves the temporal tie "in those days" found in 13:24 that appears to conflict with "but . . . after that [tribulation]" found in the same verse. "In those days" is often used to describe a coming theophanic event involving judgment or restoration (cf. Jer 3:16, 18; 5:18-19; 31:29-30; 33:14-16; Joel 2:29 [3:2 MT, LXX]; Zech 8:23; 2 Esd 4:51).[34] Yet in 13:17 and 19 it is not used as a technical term for the "last days" but simply refers to the preceding days referred to in 13:5-16 (cf. Mk 1:9; 4:35; 8:1; Mt 3:1; Lk 2:1; 4:2; 5:35; 9:36). Attempts have been made to interpret "in those days" in 13:24 as a *terminus technicus* for the last days. This would resolve the dating of the coming of the Son of Man with its preceding cosmic phenomena to a later time than the destruction of Jerusalem referred to in 13:5-23. In so doing, however, it ignores the nearest referent in 13:17 and 19 that involves the destruction of Jerusalem, instead choosing as its referent something not found in 13:1-23, the coming of the Son of Man. Although not thoroughly convincing, something like the "prophetic perspective" suggested above (see pp. 106-7) may be useful in this regard.

---

[34] Craig A. Evans, *Mark 8:27–16:20*, WBC (Nashville: Nelson, 2001), p. 327; Joel Marcus, *Mark 8–16: A New Translation with Introduction and Commentary*, AYB (New Haven, CT: Yale University Press, 2009), p. 906.

6

The Parable of the Fig Tree and the Coming Destruction of the Temple (and Jerusalem)

Mark 13:28-31

TEXT AND INTRODUCTION

²⁸"From the fig tree learn its lesson: as soon as its branch becomes tender and puts forth its leaves, you know that summer is near. ²⁹So also, when you see these things taking place, you know that he [it]¹ is near, at the very gates. ³⁰Truly I tell you, this generation will not pass away until all these things have taken place. ³¹Heaven and earth will pass away, but my words will not pass away."

The present account consists of a parable (13:28-29), actually a similitude, and two sayings (13:30 and 31). There is a shift in the message and Jesus resumes his teaching concerning the destruction of the temple and Jerusalem in 13:1-23.² There is a close literary tie between the material found in 13:28-31 and the disciples' two questions found in 13:4a and b. This is seen in the repetition of "these things" ("this" in NRSV, but *tauta* plural in Greek) in 13:4a and 13:29a and "all these things" (*tauta panta*) in 13:4b and 13:30. The readers of 13:29-30 would recall the earlier pairing of these two expressions in the same order at the beginning of this chapter. Since Jesus' answer to the disciples' twofold question concerning "these things" and "all these things" in 13:4 involves the destruction of the temple and Jerusalem, the present parable and sayings involving "these things" and "all these things" should also be interpreted as referring to the destruction of the temple and Jerusalem. Sim-

---

[1]Although *estin* can be interpreted "he/she/it is," it will be argued below that this passage is about the destruction of the temple, not the parousia of the Son of Man, so that "it is" is the better translation.
[2]Ben Witherington III, *The Gospel of Mark: A Socio-Rhetorical Commentary* (Grand Rapids: Eerdmans, 2001), p. 348.

ilarly, just as 13:24-27 introduces a new subject, the coming of the Son of Man, to the teachings concerning the destruction of the temple and Jerusalem in 13:5-23, so 13:32-37 will reintroduce this same subject, the coming of the Son of Man, to the teachings concerning the destruction of the temple and Jerusalem in 13:28-31. This completes the ABA'B' pattern described in chapter two:

A 13:5-23 The destruction of Jerusalem

B 13:24-27 The coming of the Son of Man

A' 13:28-31 The destruction of Jerusalem

B' 13:32-37 The coming of the Son of Man[3]

Two additional pieces of information concerning the destruction of Jerusalem are found in these verses. One is that the destruction of Jerusalem will take place in the lifetime of "this generation" (13:30). This statement has caused much confusion as is evident by the various ways the expression "this generation" has been interpreted. Most of the difficulty associated with this expression has been due to the misinterpretation of "these things" and "all these things" in 13:29 and 31. We will seek a holistic interpretation of these two expressions, taking into consideration the relationship of the disciples' twofold question in 13:4, Jesus' answer to these two questions in 13:5-23, and the use of "these things" and "all these things" in the present passage. This will in turn enable us to make sense of the expression "this generation" and its relationship to the events of 13:5-23 and 28-31. A final piece of information found in our passage involves the apparent end of "heaven and earth" referred to and emphasized by Jesus' "Truly I tell you" (13:31).

Mark 13:28-29: The Parable of the Fig Tree

The parable of the fig tree recalls Jesus' parabolic action in 11:12-14 and 20-21 involving the cursing of a fig tree. For Mark this parabolic action is intended to be understood as the interpretative key for determining the meaning of Jesus' cleansing of the temple. By his sandwiching the temple cleansing (11:15-19) between the two parts of the cursing of the fig tree and by adding the comment "for it was not the season for figs" (11:13), Mark intends his readers to understand this action of Jesus as a

---
[3]See pp. 43 and 49 above.

parabolic guide for interpreting the cleansing of the temple. This action is not meant to be understood primarily as an act of purification or reformation. It was on the contrary an act of judgment against the religious leadership and the temple.[4]

Why Jesus chose a "fig tree" for his example in this parable cannot be known with certainty. There are numerous suggestions: the Mount of Olives was famous not only for its olive trees but its fig trees as well;[5] Jesus wanted his hearers (and Mark his readers) to interpret the parable in light of the cursing of the fig tree in 11:11-14, 20-21; a nearby fig tree provided an immediate example for Jesus' teaching; the fig tree was one of the few deciduous trees in Palestine and the budding of the fig tree would prove an excellent example of something (summer) naturally following something else (the budding of the fig tree); and so on. The last of these seems quite possible since the change described in the fig tree takes place in April around the time of the Passover (cf. 14:12). Thus the picture part of the parable (the budding of the branches of a fig tree followed by summer) provided an excellent example for the reality part of the parable ("these things taking place" followed by "it [being] near"). With respect to the main point of comparison contained in the parable, this involves not the certainty of what is coming but its nearness.[6] As to whether the parable is meant to be understood as a sign of hope (the parousia of the Son of Man being imminent)[7] or judgment (the destruction of the temple and Jerusalem is imminent), this is not self-evident and must be determined by how 13:28-31 is interpreted. "He/it is near" is capable of being interpreted as "he" (the Son of Man) or "it" (the destruction of Jerusalem) is near. If one holds to the traditional interpretation of 13:24-27, then the referent to "is" would appear to be the coming of the Son of Man. This, however, would involve interpreting 13:29 as follows, "[When you] see the 'Son of Man coming in clouds' with great power and glory [13:26] . . . you know that

---

[4]Robert H. Stein, *Mark*, BECNT (Grand Rapids: Baker Academic, 2008), pp. 511-18.
[5]William L. Lane, *The Gospel According to Mark*, NICNT (Grand Rapids: Eerdmans, 1974), p. 479.
[6]Camille Focant, *The Gospel According to Mark: A Commentary*, trans. L. R. Keylock (Eugene, OR: Pickwick, 2012), p. 549.
[7]Joel Marcus, *Mark 8–16: A New Translation with Introduction and Commentary*, AYB (New Haven, CT: Yale University Press, 2009), p. 910.

he [the Son of Man] is near." Such a statement would be pointless.[8] On the other hand, if one interprets 13:24-27 as referring to a metaphorical description of the destruction of Jerusalem, then the referent to "he/it is near" would involve the events of A.D. 70. "At the very gates" is an idiomatic expression and essentially reinforces the "nearness" of the coming event.[9]

Mark provides several helpful, interpretative clues for understanding the parable. One involves the repetition in the same order of the expressions "these things" (*tauta*) and "all these things" (*tauta panta*) as found in 13:4. These expressions are vital elements in the disciples' questions in 13:4 and are directed at Jesus' statement concerning the destruction of the temple in 13:2, "Do you see these great buildings? Not one stone will be left here upon another; all will be thrown down." In turn Jesus' reply to the disciples in 13:5-23 is directed to the disciples' twofold question in 13:4. The references to "these things" in 13:29 and "all these things" in 13:30 clearly recall their use in 13:4 and are intended to be understood as having the same referent—the destruction of the temple and Jerusalem.[10] The answer Jesus gives in 13:5-23—which is a tightly knit unit, as the opening statement ("Then Jesus began to say to them," 13:5a) and the concluding statement ("I have already told you everything," 13:23b) indicate—makes this clear. In addition, "when you see" (*hotan idēte*) in 13:29 picks up the "when you see" (*hotan idēte*) of 13:14 and deals with the "sign" preceding the destruction of the temple and Jerusalem in the disciples' question in 13:4b and Jesus' reply that the sign will be the "abomination of desolation" (13:14). This results in the following parallel:

When you see the abomination of desolation—then flee Judea to escape the imminent destruction of Jerusalem and its associated tribulations

When you see these things [the budding of the branches of a fig tree]—you know "it" [the destruction of Jerusalem] is near

---

[8]C. E. B. Cranfield, "Thoughts on New Testament Eschatology," *Scottish Journal of Theology* 35 (1982): 502; Edward Adams, *The Stars Will Fall from Heaven: Cosmic Catastrophe in the New Testament and its World*, LNTS 347 (New York: T & T Clark, 2007), p. 165.

[9]See Joachim Jeremias, "θύρα," in *The Theological Dictionary of the New Testament*, ed. Gerhard Kittel (Grand Rapids: Eerdmans, 1982), 3:173-74.

[10]"The *these things* [his italics] of verse 29 clearly refers to the 'these things' of verse 4 and verse 8, and the 'everything' (Greek, 'all things') of verse 23, that is, the troubles that the disciples are to expect, including the destruction of Jerusalem." Larry W. Hurtado, *Mark*, NIBC (Peabody, MA: Hendrickson, 1983), p. 223; cf. also Robert H. Gundry, *Mark: A Commentary on His Apology for the Cross* (Grand Rapids: Eerdmans, 1993), p. 747.

Mark 13:30-31: "Truly, I Tell You, This Generation Will Not Pass Away Until..."

The first saying of Jesus following his parable is emphasized by "truly I tell you" (cf. 3:28; 8:12; 9:1, 41; 10:15, 29; 11:23; 12:43; 14:9, 18, 25, 30). In Judaism "truly" (*'āmēn*) was generally used to conclude a statement. Its use by Jesus to introduce a statement is unusual and emphasizes the importance of what follows. It also lends support to the authenticity of the statement. For those who interpret 13:28-31 as referring to the parousia of the Son of Man rather than the destruction of Jerusalem, this saying creates a significant problem. Taken at face value, the generation of Jesus has passed away and the parousia of the Son of Man has not taken place. The emphatic "truly I tell you" makes the apparent lack of fulfillment all the more troublesome in that it raises questions as to Jesus' credibility and trustworthiness as a teacher and prophet. Added to this is that "will not pass away" involves the strongest negation possible in Greek—the subjunctive of emphatic negation (*ou mē*).[11] Consequently, numerous attempts have been made to interpret Jesus' reference to "this generation" (*hē genea hautē*) in a way that harmonizes with the "facts." Some of these include interpreting "this generation" as referring to the continued existence of the Jewish people, the human race or the followers of Jesus, or the last generation of the end time. There are several problems with such attempts. For one, these interpretations all fly in the face of the most natural way of understanding the verse.[12] The referent of "this generation" grammatically should be the "you" whom Jesus is addressing in "Truly I tell you"—that is, the disciples. Second, everywhere else that the expression "this generation" is found in Mark (8:12 [2x], 38; cf. 9:19), it refers to Jesus' contemporaries.[13] Finally, if, as has been argued in the previous paragraph, Mark's use of "these things" and "all these things" in 13:29-30 refers back to the use of these same two expressions in 13:4, then what "this generation" will live to see is the destruction

---

[11]The subjunctive of emphatic negation (*ou mē*) is also found in 9:1, 41; 10:15; 13:19, 30; 14:25; cf. also 13:31; 14:31, which are futures of emphatic negation.
[12]Marcus, *Mark 8-16*, pp. 911-12.
[13]Cf. Lane, *Mark*, p. 480; R. T. France, *The Gospel of Mark*, NIGTC (Grand Rapids: Eerdmans, 2002), p. 539. For examples of a similar use of this expression in the other Gospels, see Mt 11:16; 12:41, 42, 45; 23:36; 24:34 (cf. also 12:39; 16:4; 17:17); Lk 7:31; 11:29, 30, 31, 32, 50, 51; 17:25; 21:32 (cf. also 9:41).

of the temple and Jerusalem foretold by Jesus in 13:2 and elaborated in 13:5-23. Consequently, the apparent problem with Jesus' statement disappears not due to unusual interpretations as to what "this generation" refers to but rather to a consistent interpretation of the expressions "these things" and "all these things" in Mark 13:4 and 29-30, and the recognition that Jesus' teachings in 13:5-23 are a clarification of his statement about the destruction of the temple and Jerusalem in 13:2.[14]

The final saying in this section containing the parable of the fig tree involves Jesus' personal guarantee of the trustworthiness of his teaching. Exactly what teaching is referred to by "my words" in 13:31 is debated. It can refer to his statement about the survival of this generation until the fulfillment of "all these things" found in the previous verse,[15] the entirety of Jesus' teaching in Mark 13 or the totality of Jesus' teachings during his ministry.[16] Certainly, Mark and his readers would assume that the last of these is at least implied, for it would be impossible for them to think that whereas the teachings of Jesus found in 13:28-30 would endure forever other teachings of Jesus would pass away. As to the contrast between the temporal, created order and Jesus' eternal words, we are reminded of Old Testament sayings contrasting the perishable nature of creation with the imperishable nature of God's word (Ps 102:25-27; Is 40:6-8; 51:6; cf. Wis 18:4; 2 Esd 9:36-37; Bar 4:1) and similar sayings of Jesus (Mt 5:18; Lk 16:17).[17] Other biblical passages that refer to the perishable nature of the present creation are Genesis 8:22; Isaiah 54:9-10; Hebrews 1:10-12; 2 Peter 3:7, 10; Revelation 6:14; 20:11; 21:1. The christological significance of Jesus' statement should be noted. His words, like the Torah, will never pass away! Whereas the LORD in the Old Testament assures Israel that his promises are as per-

---

[14]Cf. Witherington, *Mark*, p. 348: "V. 30 has been contorted in various ways and given various meanings (is it referring to this race?), but such exegetical gymnastics are unnecessary if the parable goes with vv. 3-23 rather than vv. 24-27."
[15]Craig A. Evans, *Mark 8:27–16:20*, WBC (Nashville: Nelson, 2001), p. 336.
[16]C. E. B. Cranfield, *The Gospel According to Mark,* CGTC (New York: Cambridge University Press, 1959), p. 410.
[17]Based on his assumption that the Scriptures teach the permanence of the created order, France, *Mark*, p. 540, interprets 13:31 as an *a fortiori*, "Even if heaven and earth were to pass away (and they will not), my words will never pass away." Mark 13:31, however, has no "if" introducing it. It is best, therefore, to interpret it as a simple statement: "Heaven and earth will pass away, but my words will not pass away." For a helpful discussion see Adams, *Stars Will Fall*, pp. 10-16, 252-56.

The Parable of the Fig Tree and the Coming Destruction of the Temple (and Jerusalem) 127

manent and unchangeable as the course of nature (night and day, Jer 33:20-21), Jesus states that his teachings are even more permanent and imperishable than nature itself.

SUMMARY

After Jesus' teachings concerning the coming destruction of the temple and Jerusalem (13:5-23) and the following consummation of all things by the coming of the Son of Man (13:24-27), Jesus gives the first of two explanatory parables in Mark 13:28-31. This is intimately tied to teachings on the destruction of Jerusalem by the two key expressions "these things" and "all these things" in 13:4a and 13:29 and in 13:4b and 13:30. In addition, "when you see" in 13:29 ties this section closely with the "when you see" in 13:14 that is associated with the abomination of desolation. Finally, the first question of the disciples in 13:4a, "When will [these things] be?" is answered by Jesus' statement that "this generation will not pass away until all these things have taken place" (13:30) and by his personal assurance that what he has said will be more enduring and certain than the continued existence of heaven and earth.

7

The Parable of the Watchman and the Exhortation to Be Alert for the Coming of the Son of Man

Mark 13:32-37

TEXT AND INTRODUCTION

³²"But about that day or hour no one knows, neither the angels in heaven, nor the Son, but only the Father. ³³Beware, keep alert; for you do not know when the time will come. ³⁴It is like a man going on a journey, when he leaves home and puts his slaves in charge, each with his work, and commands the doorkeeper to be on the watch. ³⁵Therefore, keep awake—for you do not know when the master of the house will come, in the evening, or at midnight, or at cockcrow, or at dawn, ³⁶or else he may find you asleep when he comes suddenly. ³⁷And what I say to you I say to all: Keep awake."

There is debate as to whether Mark 13:32 is best understood as the conclusion of 13:28-31[1] or the introduction to 13:33-37.[2] It is best to understand it as beginning the final section of Mark 13 for several reasons. First, the call to watchfulness in 13:33-37 is based on the inability to know the time of the coming of the Son of Man (13:32). In contrast the disciples (note the "you" in 13:28-30) are to watch for a sign that reveals when "these things" and "all these

---

[1]Craig A. Evans, *Mark 8:27-16:20*, WBC (Nashville: Nelson, 2001), pp. 333-37; Joel Marcus, *Mark 8-16: A New Translation with Introduction and Commentary*, AYB (New Haven, CT: Yale University Press, 2009), pp. 910-18; Camille Focant, *The Gospel According to Mark: A Commentary*, trans. L. R. Keylock (Eugene, OR: Pickwick, 2012), pp. 548-52.
[2]William L. Lane, *The Gospel According to Mark*, NICNT (Grand Rapids: Eerdmans, 1974), pp. 480-84; Morna D. Hooker, *The Gospel According to Saint Mark*, BNTC (Peabody, MA: Hendrickson, 1991), pp. 322-24; James R. Edwards, *The Gospel According to Mark*, PNTC (Grand Rapids: Eerdmans, 2002), pp. 406-9; R. T. France, *The Gospel of Mark*, NIGTC (Grand Rapids: Eerdmans, 2002), pp. 541-46; most English translations (RSV, NRSV, NIV, ESV, NAB).

things" (13:29-30) take place.[3] Thus the universal ignorance of "that day," except for God, is better suited to the "signlessness" of 13:33-37 than the command to look for the sign of the abomination of desolation foretelling the imminence of Jerusalem's destruction in 13:4 and 14 and the analogous sign of the coming summer in the parable of the fig tree in 13:28. In contrast the coming of the homeowner in 13:35 is not preceded by any "sign" whatsoever. Second, "the resounding certainty"[4] of "Truly I tell you, this generation will not pass away" (13:30-31) stands in striking contrast to Jesus not knowing "that day or hour" in 13:32. Third, "But about" (*peri de*) in 13:32 is best understood here as elsewhere in the New Testament as introducing a switch in subject. This is especially clear in 1 Corinthians 7:1, 25; 8:1; 12:1; 16:1, 12; 1 Thessalonians 4:9; 5:1.[5] Fourth, in this final section of Mark 13 we find a switch from the theme of the destruction of the temple and Jerusalem (13:1-4, 5-23, 28-31) back to the theme of the coming of the Son of Man (13:24-27). The most suitable antecedent for "that day" in 13:32 is the coming of the Son of Man (13:24-27) "in those days, after that suffering" (13:24). Fifth, Matthew clearly associates Jesus' saying in 13:32 (Mt 24:36) with the coming of the Son of Man in 24:37-44 (see especially vv. 37, 42, 44). This is evident in that "But about that day and hour no one knows . . . but only the Father" (24:36) is followed by "for as . . ." (24:37-44) that deals with the coming of the Son of Man. Finally, it should be observed that no other major section in Mark 13 (cf. 13:1, 5, 14, 24 and 28) begins with an exhortation. Thus it would be quite unusual for the final section to begin with the exhortation of 13:33. As a result it is best to understand 13:32 as introducing the material in 13:33-37 rather than as concluding 13:28-31.[6]

---

[3]Hooker, *Mark*, p. 322.
[4]France, *Mark*, p. 541.
[5]Jeffrey A. Gibbs, *Jerusalem and Parousia: Jesus' Eschatological Discourse in Matthew's Gospel* (St. Louis: Concordia Academic Press, 2000), pp. 172-73, argues that "but about" in the Matthean parallel (24:36) reaches back and responds to the second part of the disciples' twofold question in 24:3. In Matthew this may be correct. However, in Mark 13:32 "but about" introduces a new subject contrasting the destruction of the temple in 13:28-31 and recalls not the disciples' second question in 13:4 but the preceding passage (13:24-27) in which Jesus teaches concerning the coming of the Son of Man.
[6]Although in the Old Testament "in those days" can serve as a synonym for "in that day" (cf. Joel 3:18; cf. also "the day of the Lord" with Joel 2:1-2, 32; 3:14), in Mark 13 these two expressions signify different events. "In those days" in 13:17, 19, 24 (cf. also 13:20) does not refer to a specific day, because no particular day is singled out in 13:5-24. Even 13:14 does not single out a specific day as much as a sign "when you see [become aware of] the abomination of desolation [desolating sacrilege, NRSV] set up where it ought not to be."

Linguistically, this section is held together and structured around three plural, imperative phrases: "beware, keep alert" (13:33), "keep awake" (13:35) and "keep awake" (13:37). It consists of an introductory statement concerning the unknowable nature of the time of the Son of Man's coming (13:32); a twofold warning not to be caught off guard but to be alert for that event becuase of its unknowable nature (13:33); an illustrative parable and its interpretation (13:34-36); and a final warning to be alert (13:37).

Having given a parabolic illustration concerning the "when" of the temple's destruction in 13:28-31, Jesus makes a statement concerning the inability to know the time of "that day"—the parousia of the Son of Man—and an explanatory comment of the consequences of this. He introduces this by a change in theme from "these things" and "all these things" (13:4, 29-30) concerning the destruction of the temple and Jerusalem to "that day or hour" after that tribulation/suffering (13:24) when the Son of Man comes in clouds with great power and glory (13:26) to gather his elect (13:27).

MARK 13:32-33: NO ONE KNOWS BUT ONLY THE FATHER

Although some scholars have denied the authenticity of Mark 13:32,[7] "its offence seals its genuineness."[8] The difficulty that this verse created for the early church makes it extremely unlikely that the saying would have been created by the early Christian community.[9] The exact referent of "that day" is debated. Some have suggested that the expression is a synonym for "in

---

[7]Rudolf Bultmann, *The History of the Synoptic Tradition*, trans. John Marsh (New York: Harper, 1963), p. 123.

[8]Vincent Taylor, *The Gospel According to St. Mark* (London: Macmillan, 1952), p. 522. Cf. John P. Meier, *A Marginal Jew: Rethinking the Historical Jesus* (New York: Doubleday, 1991), p. 169, who points out that the authenticity of this saying is supported by its fulfilling "the criterion of embarrassment." This criterion argues that the embarrassment this saying created for the Christology of the early church makes it very unlikely that the early church would have created it. Whether 13:32 was an independent saying whose present location is due to Mark (George R. Beasley-Murray, *Jesus and the Last Days: The Interpretation of the Olivet Discourse* [Peabody, MA: Hendrickson, 1993], p. 453) is not especially relevant for our discussion. It has been argued that 13:30 and 13:32 could not have been said one after the other by Jesus, but if it was possible for Mark to place them "one after the other," it might also have made sense for Jesus as well.

[9]This difficulty can be seen by Luke's omission of this verse in his Gospel, the omission of "nor the Son" in various manuscripts of the Matthean parallel in 24:36 (it is not found in ℵ¹ L W f¹ vg. syr.) and the various attempts of the early church to explain away the apparent ignorance of the Son of God. See Francis X. Gumerlock, "Mark 13:32 and Christ's Supposed Ignorance: Four Patristic Solutions," *Trinity Journal* 28 (2007): 205-13. It should be noted that being ignorant of something is not the same as teaching error.

those days" found in 13:24. These expressions are not the same, however. "In those days" refers to a period of time in 13:17, 19 and 24 (cf. also v. 20) involving the destruction of Jerusalem and the events leading up to it. This includes the appearance of the abomination of desolation and the subsequent flight from the city. "That day," on the other hand, refers in the parable of 13:34-35 to an event, the sudden appearance of the homeowner, not a period of time. In contrast to the previous parable in which the gradual swelling of the fig trees warns of the coming of the destruction of Jerusalem, this parable speaks of the suddenness and surprise of "that day." It should also be noted that the expression "that day" is a standard Old Testament expression for a theophanic event (Is 2:11-12, 20; 34:8; Jer 46:10; Ezek 13:5; Joel 3:18; Amos 5:18-20; 8:3, 9, 13; 9:11; Mic 4:6; 5:10; 7:12; Zeph 1:7-18; 3:16; Zech 9:16; 14:1-21). The interchangeableness of such terms as "that day," "the day of" and "the day when" is witnessed to by such passages as Isaiah 2:11-22 (esp. 12, 17, 20); Jeremiah 46:10; Ezekiel 7:7-27 (esp. 7, 10, 12, 19); 30:2-3. In the New Testament we find similar expressions (1 Thess 5:2, 4; 2 Thess 2:2, 3) used to describe the parousia of the Son of Man. Thus this expression in 13:32 was probably familiar to both Jesus' hearers and Mark's readers, and Mark's readers would have interpreted it in light of their expectation and hope of the coming of the Son of Man.

The ascending order of "no one," "the angels in heaven," "the Son" and "the Father"[10] involves a high Christology indeed. Jesus is not only distinct from humans and angels; he is superior to them and is uniquely God's Son. Earlier in the parable of the wicked tenants, he is distinguished from God's servants, the prophets, and is God's "beloved" Son (12:6). Although a prophet, Jesus cannot simply be categorized a "prophet." He is the Son! This does not in any way belittle the prophets, but simply indicates the superiority and uniqueness of Jesus as the Son of God.[11] For a similar unqualified reference to Jesus being "the Son," compare 12:6 and the so-called Johannine thunderbolt in Matthew 11:27/Luke 10:22.

The first warning in 13:33 consists of the exhortations to "beware" and "keep alert." Although a number of manuscripts add "and pray" (*kai*

---

[10]France, *Mark*, p. 543.
[11]This distinction is found throughout the New Testament—cf., e.g., Heb 1:1-9; Jn 3:16-17, 35, 36 (2x); 5:19 (2x), 20, 21.

proseuchesthe),[12] its omission from manuscripts B and D is hard to explain if it were part of the original manuscript. Most likely it is a later addition to Mark 13:33 due to its presence in 14:38 which contains the warning to "keep awake and pray." It has been argued that 13:33 was originally an isolated saying in the Gospel tradition (an *Einzelwort*) and that Mark added it to introduce the following parable of the watchman and that Matthew added it to conclude the parable of the ten maidens in Matthew 25:13.[13] All this is quite speculative and of little consequence in seeking to understand the present form of our Markan text.

Mark 13:34: The Parable of the Watchman

The parable, or similitude, of the watchful doorkeeper consists of an incomplete sentence in Greek, and the reader is expected to supply "It is" to make "like a man going on a journey, when he leaves home and puts his slaves in charge, each with his work, and commands the doorkeeper to be on the watch" into a complete sentence. The existence of similar parables such as "the watchful servants" (Lk 12:35-38), "the thief breaking in" (Lk 12:39-40/Mt 24:43-44), the "faithful and wise servants" (Lk 12:42-46/Mt 24:45-51) and the "pounds" (Lk 19:12-27/Mt 25:14-30) has raised questions as to the relationship of these parables and whether our present parable may be a variant of one of them. Numerous attempts have also been made to reconstruct the original form of Jesus' parable. Again we must remind ourselves of the goal of our research. Since our goal is to understand the meaning of the present form of the parable in Mark, we must leave aside the mining of this parable for information about the historical Jesus and the history of the transmission of this tradition.[14]

The present parable supplies no explanation of why the man was going on a journey. It was not thought important or necessary by Jesus or Mark in order to understand the parable. The parable has often been interpreted as an allegory in which the man represents Jesus, the journey represents the ascension of Jesus into heaven, the return represents the parousia of the Son of Man, the servants represent disciples/believers and the doorkeeper rep-

---

[12] So ℵ A C L W θ f¹ f¹³ *lat. syr.*
[13] Beasley-Murray, *Jesus and the Last Days*, p. 301.
[14] See chapter one above.

resents the apostles (cf. John 10:3). The genre of "parable" (*mašal* in the Old Testament; *parabolē* in the New Testament) in the Bible is a broad one that includes proverbs, similes, metaphors, riddles, similitudes, story and example parables, and allegories. Allegories should be interpreted allegorically, but parables should not be "allegorized."[15] In a parable a basic analogy is intended, and the details are generally meant to add color and interest to the story. They are not meant to be searched for an allegorical meaning. Thus our parable possesses a basic analogy in which the picture part of the parable corresponds to a reality part. The basic picture involves the need for a doorkeeper to be prepared for the coming of a man (the master of the house, 13:35) at an unknown time. The reality to which this picture refers involves the Son of Man (13:26), his coming (the parousia) and a doorkeeper (the church or "you" of 13:37). There is no need or reason to allegorize such details as the journey, the servants or the work given to them. We should refrain from interpreting these details allegorically simply because we can or because the allegorical meaning given to them fits standard Christian theology or our own theological interests. Rather we should do so only if we must. In light of the allegorical excesses associated with past interpretations of the parables, we should be cautious about finding allegorical significance in various details in this and other parables. One should concentrate rather on the basic elements of the picture and seek to understand the reality to which they point.

Mark 13:35-36: The Application of the Parable to Mark's Readers

The interpretation of the parable picks up the command given to a doorkeeper to "be on the watch" (*grēgore*, 13:34) with an injunction directed to the readers to "keep awake" (*grēgoreite*, 13:35) and the explanation "for you do not know when the master of the house will come." The explanation picks up the opening statement of the section concerning the unknowability of "that day" (13:32) when the Son of Man comes. The emphasis of the parable is not that the return of the Son of Man is uncertain or unexpected but rather that it is unpredictable and the time is unknown (cf. Mt

---

[15]See Robert H. Stein, "The Genre of the Parables," in *The Challenge of Jesus' Parables*, ed. Richard N. Longenecker (Grand Rapids: Eerdmans, 2000), pp. 46-47.

24:45-51; 25:1-13; Lk 12:36-40; cf. also Mt 25:14-30; Lk 19:12-27). This is further emphasized by its being described as coming during one of the four watches of the night: evening (*opse*) 6–9 p.m.; midnight (*mesonuktion*) 9–12 p.m.; cockcrow (*alektorophōnias*) 12–3 a.m.; or dawn (*prōi*) 3–6 a.m. Three of these watches are mentioned, perhaps intentionally, in 14:17 and 15:42 ("evening"), 14:72 ("at [the] moment the cock crowed") and 15:1 ("morning" or "dawn"),[16] and the warning not to be found sleeping prepares for 14:37. The reference to four watches betrays a Roman reckoning of time (cf. 6:48, "fourth watch of the night"; Acts 12:4; *Ant.* 5.223; 18.356; *J.W.* 5.510-11). A Jewish reckoning of time involved three watches in the night (Judg 7:19; *Jubilees* 49:10-12; *b. Ber.* 3b).

Mark 13:37: The Universal Call to Be Prepared for the Parousia of the Son of Man

The final command to "keep awake" (*grēgoreite*) serves as a conclusion for 13:32-37 and the entire chapter as well. In contrast to earlier exhortations in 13:5-23 and 28-31 (no exhortations are found in 13:24-27) that are addressed by Jesus to his disciples and followers in Judea (13:14), the final exhortation extends beyond this "you" (cf. 13:5, 7, 9, 11, 13, 14, 18, 21, 23, 28-30, 33, 35, 36, 37) to "all"! Here the exhortation looks past the "you" in Judea facing the destruction of Jerusalem. It looks to the church in Mark's day and subsequent readers of the Gospel.

The command here focuses primarily on "that day" as a threat, and the need to prepare oneself for the sudden coming of the Son of Man at a time unknown to all but God. Elsewhere there is an emphasis on the positive, joyous anticipation of those who are awake and love the coming of the Son of Man (2 Tim 4:8). This is emphasized in the Lord's Prayer ("Your kingdom come," Mt 6:10/Lk 11:2) and by the Aramaic prayer repeated in the Gentile church in Corinth (*Marana tha*, 1 Cor 16:22) and its Greek translation *erchou kurie Iēsou* (Come, Lord Jesus!) in Revelation 22:20. This "blessed hope" (Tit 2:13), longingly awaited, was a source of great encouragement and anticipation (1 Thess 4:18; 5:11) for grieving Christians as they looked

---

[16]Troy W. Martin, "Watch During the Watches (Mark 13:35)," *JBL* 120 (2001): 685-701, points out that, although the fourfold designation of the watches of the night reveals a Roman reckoning of time, the names given to the watches are Jewish.

forward to a joyous reunion with relatives and friends who had preceded them in death (1 Thess 4:17).

The exhortation to "keep awake" indicates that the warnings against apocalyptic preoccupation and frenzy in 13:5-8 and 21-23 are not meant to weaken the blessed hope of the parousia but rather to encourage watching, looking forward to and praying for the coming of the Son of Man. The longing for the blessed hope of the appearing of our God and Savior Jesus Christ is not primarily a characteristic of certain fanatics on the fringe of the Christian community but has been, is and will continue to be at the heart of the Christian community's hope and longing. This is why the Christian community has, is and will continue to pray, "Your kingdom come" and "*Marana tha.*"

"Scoffers may disparage as dreamers people whose attention is focused on future events (cf. Gen 37:19; 2 Pet 3:3-4; cf. Jude 8), but Mark implies that it is these dreamers who really have their eyes peeled. The 'realists,' on the other hand—who think that the world will continue indefinitely on its accustomed course—are simply dreaming."[17]

---

[17]Marcus, *Mark 8–16*, pp. 922-23.

8

An Interpretative Translation of Mark 13

¹As Jesus was leaving the temple, one of his disciples said to him, "Teacher, look! Aren't the stones and buildings of the temple magnificent!" ²In response Jesus replied, "You see these great buildings? [Within your lifetime (13:30) they will be totally destroyed and] not a single stone will remain attached to another! They will all be thrown down!" ³As Jesus was sitting with his disciples Peter, James, John and Andrew on the Mount of Olives facing the temple, they asked him privately, ⁴"Tell us, when will *these things* take place, and what will be the sign preceding all *these things* [that will warn us that the destruction of the temple is about to take place]?"

⁵[In response to the disciples' twofold question concerning the time of the temple's destruction and the sign preceding it] Jesus began to say to them, "Be on your guard and do not let anyone deceive you. ⁶Many [deceivers] will come claiming to be the Christ and saying, 'I am the Messiah!' and they will deceive many people. ⁷And whenever you hear reports of wars and rumors of wars do not be alarmed by this! It is necessary that such things take place, but these are not signs of the [imminent destruction and] end [of the temple]. ⁸For nations will go to war with other nations and kingdoms will go to war with other kingdoms. There will be earthquakes occurring in various places and famines as well. [These are also not signs of the temple's imminent destruction.] These are but the beginning of events preceding its destruction [but they are not the sign indicating its imminence].

⁹"But *you*, be on your guard, for they will deliver you over to Jewish courts [for trial] and you will be beaten in synagogues, and you will be brought for trial before governors and kings because of your allegiance to me [and this will serve as an opportunity] to bear witness to them. ¹⁰And it is necessary that the

gospel be preached first in all the nations [before the temple is destroyed]. ¹¹And whenever they deliver you over for trial, do not worry beforehand about what you should say, but say whatever God gives to you at that hour, for it will not be your words and thoughts that you speak but the words and thoughts that the Holy Spirit has given you! ¹²And [things will become so bad that] a brother will even betray his own brother and deliver him over to [trial resulting in his] death, a father will deliver over his own child [to death], and children will rise up against their parents leading to their death! ¹³You will be hated by everyone for being my disciples [as I have already told you (8:34-38)], but the one who remains faithful until death, this person will be saved!

¹⁴"But [concerning the sign you asked about] when you see the abomination of desolation standing [in the temple] where he ought not to be, you who are reading this Gospel make sure that you understand this [in light of the abomination of desolation referred to in the yearly celebration of Hanukkah, the Feast of Lights]. Then you who are in Judea must flee immediately to the mountains! ¹⁵If you are relaxing on the roof of your house, do not come down and enter your house to take anything with you! [Flee while you still can!] ¹⁶If you are working in the field, do not return home to get your coat. [Flee while you still can!] ¹⁷And woe to those poor souls who are pregnant and nursing children in those days [for whom flight is more difficult]! ¹⁸Pray that this does not happen in winter [when flight is more difficult], ¹⁹for those days will bring such tribulation as has never been seen on the earth from the beginning of creation that God created until now and will never be again. ²⁰And if the Lord did not shorten those days [of tribulation], no one would be saved! But for the sake of his elect, whom he has elected, he has shortened those days. ²¹And then if anyone should say to you, 'Look, here is the Christ' [or] 'Look, there [he is],' do not believe it. ²²For false christs and false prophets will appear and perform signs and wonders in order to lead astray, if possible, the elect. ²³But *you* be on your guard! I have told you *all things* beforehand.

²⁴"But in those days after that terrible tribulation [associated with the destruction of the temple and Jerusalem] God will cause

> the sun to become dark,
> and the moon not to give its light,
> ²⁵and the stars to fall from heaven,
> and the powers of heaven to shake.

²⁶"And then [the whole world] will see the Son of Man coming in clouds with great power and glory! ²⁷Then he will send the angels and gather his elect from the four corners of the earth, from the end of the earth to the end of heaven.

²⁸"Learn from the fig tree the following parable: as soon as its branch becomes tender and sprouts leaves, you know that summer is near. ²⁹So likewise, when you see *these things* [in particular the appearance of the abomination of desolation] taking place, you know that it [the destruction of the temple you asked about] is at the very door. ³⁰I am telling you the truth, this present generation will in no way die off before *all these things* [you asked about] will have taken place! ³¹Heaven and earth will pass away, but the words that I have told you will never, ever pass away!

³²"But now about that day or hour [of the coming of the Son of Man]—no human being knows this. Not even the angels in heaven, nor I, God's Son, know this. Only the Father knows it! ³³Therefore be on your guard and keep awake, because you do not know the time [of the Son of Man's coming]. ³⁴It is like when a man leaves his home on a journey. Before going he gives each of his servants authority for their specific task and commands the doorkeeper to watch [for his return]. ³⁵You watch therefore for you do not know exactly when the Lord of the house is coming. It may be at evening [6–9 p.m.], midnight [9–12 p.m.], cockcrow [12–3 a.m.] or dawn [3–6 a.m.], ³⁶and you do not want to be found sleeping when he suddenly comes. ³⁷What I am saying to you I am saying to all: 'Watch!'"

Bibliography

Adams, Edward. "The Coming of the Son of Man in Mark's Gospel." *Tyndale Bulletin* 56, no. 2 (2005): 39-61.

―――. *The Stars Will Fall from Heaven: Cosmic Catastrophe in the New Testament and Its World*. LNTS 347. New York: T & T Clark, 2007.

Allison, Dale C., Jr. "Jesus & the Victory of Apocalyptic." In *Jesus & the Restoration of Israel: A Critical Assessment of N. T. Wright's Jesus and the Victory of God*, pp. 126-41. Edited by Carey C. Newman. Downers Grove, IL: InterVarsity Press, 1999.

Ambrozic, A. M. *The Hidden Kingdom: A Redaction-Critical Study of the References to the Kingdom of God in Mark's Gospel*. CBQMS 2. Washington, DC: Catholic Biblical Association of America, 1972.

Aune, David E. *Apocalypticism, Prophecy, and Magic in Early Christianity: Collected Essays*. Grand Rapids: Baker Academic, 2008.

Bahat, Dan. "Jerusalem Down Under: Tunneling Along Herod's Temple Mount Wall." *BAR* 21, no. 6 (1995): 30-47.

Balabanski, Vicky. *Eschatology in the Making: Mark, Matthew, and the Didache*. SNTSMS 97. Cambridge: University Press, 1997.

Barnes, T. D. "The Fragments of Tacitus' *Histories*." *Classical Philology* 72 (1977): 24-31.

Beasley-Murray, George R. *Jesus and the Last Days: The Interpretation of the Olivet Discourse*. Peabody, MA: Hendrikson, 1993.

Beavis, Mary Ann. *Mark*. Paideia. Grand Rapids: Baker Academic, 2011.

Bengel, Johann Albrecht. *Gnomon of the New Testament*. 2 vols. New York: Sheldon, 1862.

Bird, Michael F. "The Markan Community, Myth or Maze? Bauckham's *The Gospel for All Christians* Revisited." *JTS* 57 (2006): 474-86.

Black, C. Clifton. *Mark*. ANTC. Nashville: Abingdon, 2011.

Bock, Darrell L. *Acts*. BECNT. Grand Rapids: Baker Academic, 2007.

Boring, M. Eugene. *Mark*. NTL. Louisville: Westminster John Knox, 2006.

Bornkamm, Günther. *Jesus of Nazareth*. Translated by I. McLusky et al. New York: Harper, 1960.

Brooks, James A. *Mark*. NAC. Nashville: Broadman, 1991.

Brown, Colin. "Quest of the Historical Jesus." In *Dictionary of Jesus and the Gospels*, rev. ed., pp. 718-56. Edited by Joel B. Green. Downers Grove, IL: IVP Academic, 2013.

Bultmann, Rudolf. *The History of the Synoptic Tradition*, 2nd ed. Translated by John Marsh. New York: Harper, 1968.

Caird, G. B. *The Language and Imagery of the Bible*. Philadelphia: Westminister, 1980.

Chanikuzhy, Jacob. *Jesus, the Eschatological Temple: An Exegetical Study of Jn 2,13-22 in the Light of the Pre-70 C.E. Eschatological Temple Hopes and the Synoptic Temple Action*. CBET. Leuven: Peeters, 2012.

Charlesworth, James H., ed. *The Old Testament Pseudepigrapha*. 2 vols. New York: Doubleday, 1985.

Collins, Adela Y. "The Apocalyptic Rhetoric of Mark 13 in Historical Context." *Biblical Research* 41 (1996): 5-36.

———. *The Beginning of the Gospel: Probings of Mark in Context*. Minneapolis: Fortress, 1992.

———. "The Eschatological Discourse of Mark 13." In *The Four Gospels*, pp. 1125-40. Edited by F. van Segbroeck et al. BETL. Leuven: Leuven University Press, 1992.

———. *Mark: A Commentary*. Hermeneia. Minneapolis: Fortress, 2007.

Collins, Adela Y., and John J. Collins. *King and Messiah as Son of God: Divine, Human, and Angelic Messianic Figures in Biblical and Related Literature*. Grand Rapids: Eerdmans, 2008.

Coloni, T. *Jésus Christ et les croyances messianiques de son Temps*, 2nd ed. Strasbourg: Treuttel et Würtz, 1864.

Cranfield, C. E. B. *The Gospel According to Mark*. Edited by C. F. D. Moule. CGTC. New York: Cambridge University Press, 1959.

———. "Thoughts on New Testament Eschatology." *Scottish Journal of Theology* 35 (1982): 497-512.

Davies, W. D., and Dale C. Allison. *A Critical and Exegetical Commentary on the Gospel According to Saint Matthew*. ICC. 3 vols. Edinburgh: T & T Clark, 1991.

Dean, J. E., ed. *Epiphanius's Treatise on Weights and Measures: Syriac Version*. Studies in Ancient Oriental Civilization 11. Chicago: University of Chicago Press, 1935.

Deppe, Dean B. "Charting the Future or a Perspective of the Present? The Paraenetic Purpose of Mark 13." *CTJ* 41 (2006): 89-101.
Donahue, John R. *Are You the Christ? The Trial Narrative in the Gospel of Mark*. SBLDS 10. Missoula, MT: Society of Biblical Literature, 1973.
Donahue, John R., and Daniel J. Harrington. *The Gospel of Mark*. SP. Collegeville, MN: Liturgical Press, 2002.
Edwards, James R. *The Gospel According to Mark*. PNTC. Grand Rapids: Eerdmans, 2002.
Ernst, Josef. *Das Evangelium nach Markus*. RNT. Regensburg: Pustet, 1981.
Evans, Craig A. *Fabricating Jesus: How Modern Scholars Distort the Gospels*. Downers Grove, IL: InterVarsity Press, 2006.
———. *Mark 8:27-16:20*. WBC. Nashville: Nelson, 2001.
———. "Predictions of the Destruction of the Herodian Temple in the Pseudepigrapha, Qumran Scrolls, and Related Texts." *Journal for the Study of the Pseudepigrapha* 10 (1992): 89-147.
Focant, Camille. *The Gospel According to Mark: A Commentary*. Translated by L. R. Keylock. Eugene, OR: Pickwick, 2012.
Ford, Desmond. *The Abomination of Desolation in Biblical Eschatology*. Washington, DC: University Press of America, 1979.
Fowler, Robert M. *"Let the Reader Understand": Reader-Response Criticism and the Gospel of Mark*. Minneapolis: Augsburg, 1991.
France, R. T. *Jesus and the Old Testament: His Application of the Old Testament Passages to Himself and His Mission*. Downers Grove, IL: InterVarsity Press, 1971.
———. *The Gospel of Mark*. NIGTC. Grand Rapids: Eerdmans, 2002.
Funk, Robert W., and Roy W. Hoover. *The Five Gospels: The Search for the Authentic Words of Jesus*. New York: Poleridge, 1993.
Gaston, Lloyd. *No Stone on Another: Studies in the Significance of the Fall of Jerusalem in the Synoptic Gospels*. Leiden: Brill, 1970.
Geddert, Timothy J. *Watchwords: Mark 13 in Markan Eschatology*. JSNTSS 26. Sheffield: Sheffield Academic Press, 1989.
Gibbs, Jeffrey A. *Jerusalem and Parousia: Jesus' Eschatological Discourse in Matthew's Gospel*. St. Louis: Concordia Academic Press, 2000.
Gnilka, Joachim. *Das Evangelium nach Markus (Mk 8,27-16,20)*. EKKNT 2/2. Zurich: Benzinger, 1979.
Gould, Ezra Palmer. *A Critical and Exegetical Commentary on the Gospel According to St. Mark*. ICC. New York: T & T Clark, 1896.

Gray, Timothy C. *The Temple in the Gospel of Mark: A Study in Its Narrative Role.* Grand Rapids: Baker Academic, 2010.

Grayston, Kenneth. "The Study of Mark XIII." *BJRL* 56 (1974): 371-87.

Gumerlock, Francis X. "Mark 13:32 and Christ's Supposed Ignorance: Four Patristic Solutions." *Trinity Journal* 28 (2007): 205-13.

Gundry, Robert H. *Mark: A Commentary on His Apology for the Cross.* Grand Rapids: Eerdmans, 1993.

Hare, Douglas R. A. *The Theme of Jewish Persecution of Christians in the Gospel According to St. Matthew.* SNTSMS 6. New York: Cambridge University Press, 1967.

Hatina, Thomas R. "The Focus of Mark 13:24-27—The Parousia or the Destruction of the Temple." *BBR* 6 (1996): 43-66.

———. *In Search of a Context: The Function of Scripture in Mark's Narrative.* JSNTSS 232. Sheffield: Sheffield Academic Press, 2002.

Hendriksen, William. *Exposition of the Gospel According to Mark.* NTC. Grand Rapids: Baker, 1975.

Hengel, Martin. *Studies in the Gospel of Mark.* Translated by John Bowden. Philadelphia: Fortress, 1985.

———. "Tasks in New Testament Scholarship." *BBR* 6 (1996): 67-86.

Hooker, Morna D. *The Gospel According to Saint Mark.* BNTC. Peabody, MA: Hendrickson, 1991.

———. "Trial and Tribulation in Mark XIII." *BJRL* 65 (1982): 78-99.

Hurtado, Larry H. *Mark.* NIBC. Peabody, MA: Hendrickson, 1983.

Jeremias, Joachim. "Θύρα." In *The Theological Dictionary of the New Testament*, 3:173-74. Edited by G. Kittel. Grand Rapids: Eerdmans, 1982.

Kähler, Martin. *The So-Called Historical Jesus and the Historic Biblical Christ.* Translated by Carl E. Braatan. Philadelphia: Fortress, 1964.

Käsemann, Ernst. "Das Problem des Historischen Jesus." *Zeitschrift für Theologie und Kirche* 51 (1954): 125-53.

———. "The Problem of the Historical Jesus." In *Essays on New Testament Themes*, pp. 15-47. Translated by W. J. Montague. SBT 41. London: SCM Press, 1964.

Kelber, Werner H. *The Kingdom in Mark: A New Place and a New Time.* Philadelphia: Fortress, 1974.

Lambrecht, Jan. *Die Redaktion der Markus-Apocalypse: Literarische Analyse und Strukturuntersuchung.* AnBib 28. Rome: Päpstliches Bibelinstitut, 1967.

Lane, William L. *The Gospel According to Mark: The English Text with Introduction, Exposition, and Notes.* NICNT. Grand Rapids: Eerdmans, 1974.

Lightfoot, Robert Henry. *Locality and Doctrine in the Gospels*. New York: Harper, 1937.

Lohmeyer, Ernst. *Galiläa und Jerusalem*. FRLANT. Göttingen: Vandenhoeck & Ruprecht, 1937.

Lührmann, Dieter. *Das Markusevangelium*. HTKNT 3. Tübingen: Mohr Siebeck, 1987.

Manson, T. W. *The Sayings of Jesus as Recorded in the Gospels According to St. Matthew and St. Luke: Arranged with Introduction and Commentary*. Grand Rapids: Eerdmans, 1957.

Marcus, Joel. "The Jewish War and the *Sitz im Leben* of Mark." *JBL* 111 (1992): 441-62.

———. *Mark 1–8: A New Translation with Introduction and Commentary*. AYB. New Haven, CT: Yale University Press, 2002.

———. *Mark 8–16: A New Translation with Introduction and Commentary*. AYB. New Haven, CT: Yale University Press, 2009.

Martin, Troy W. "Watch During the Watches (Mark 13:35)." *JBL* 120 (2001): 685-701.

Marxsen, Willi. *Mark the Evangelist: Studies on the Redaction History of the Gospel*. Translated by James Boyce et al. Nashville: Abingdon, 1969.

McKenna, Megan. *On Your Mark: Reading Mark in the Shadow of the Cross*. Maryknoll, NY: Orbis, 2006.

McKnight, Scot. *A New Vision for Israel: The Teachings of Jesus in National Context*. Grand Rapids: Eerdmans, 1999.

Meier, John P. *A Marginal Jew: Rethinking the Historical Jesus*. New York: Doubleday, 1991.

———. "The Present State of the 'Third Quest' for the Historical Jesus: Loss and Gain." *Biblica* 80 (1999): 459-87.

Merkle, Benjamin L. "Who Will Be Left Behind? Rethinking the Meaning of Matthew 24:40-41 and Luke 17:34-35." *WTJ* 72 (2010): 169-79.

Moloney, Francis J. *Glory Not Dishonor: Reading John 13–21*. Minneapolis: Fortress, 1998.

———. *The Gospel of Mark: A Commentary*. Peabody, MA: Hendrickson, 2002.

Neill, Stephen, and Tom Wright. *The Interpretation of the New Testament 1861–1986*. 2nd ed. New York: Oxford University Press, 1988.

Nineham, D. E. *Saint Mark*. PGC. Baltimore: Penguin, 1963.

Painter, John. *Mark's Gospel: Worlds in Conflict*. Edited by John Court. NTR. London: Routledge, 1997.

Paulus, Heinrich E. G. *Das Leben Jesu als Grundlage einer reinen Geschichte des Urchristentums*. Heidelberg: C. F. Winter, 1828.

Perkins, Larry. "'Let the Reader Understand': A Contextual Interpretation of Mark 13:14." *BBR* 16, no. 1 (2006): 95-104.

Pesch, Rudolf. *Das Markusevangelium, Part 2: Kommentur zu Mark 8,27–16:20*. 2nd edition. HTKNT 2. Freiburg: Herder, 1981.

———. *Naherwartungen: Tradition und Redaktion in Mk 13*. KBANT. Düsseldorf: Patmos-Verlag, 1968.

Pitre, Brant. *Jesus, the Tribulation, and the End of the Exile: Restoration Eschatology and the Origin of the Atonement*. Grand Rapids: Baker Academic, 2005.

Porter, Stanley E. *The Criteria for Authenticity in Historical-Jesus Research: Previous Discussions and New Proposals*. JSNTSS 191. Sheffield: Sheffield Academic Press, 2000.

Reimarus, Hermann Samuel. *Reimarus: Fragments*. Edited by Charles H. Talbert. Translated by R. S. Fraser. Lives of Jesus. Philadelphia: Fortress, 1970.

Robinson, James M. *A New Quest for the Historical Jesus and Other Essays*. SBT 15. London: SCM Press, 1959.

Sanders, E. P. *The Tendencies of the Synoptic Tradition*. SNTSMS 9. New York: Cambridge University Press, 1969.

Schnabel, Eckhard. *40 Questions About the End Times*. Grand Rapids: Kregel, 2011.

Schweitzer, Albert. *The Quest of the Historical Jesus: A Critical Study of Its Progress from Reimarus to Wrede*. Translated by W. Montgomery. New York: Macmillan, 1906.

Snodgrass, Klyne R. "Parables." In *The Dictionary of Jesus and the Gospels*, pp. 591-601. Edited by Joel B. Green and Scot McKnight. Downers Grove, IL: InterVarsity Press, 1992.

Snow, Robert S. "Let the Reader Understand: Mark's Use of Jeremiah 7 in Mark 13:14." *BBR* 21, no. 4 (2011): 467-77.

Sowers, Sidney. "The Circumstances and Recollection of the Pella Flight." *Theologische Zeitschrift* 26 (1970): 305-20.

Stein, Robert H. *A Basic Guide to Interpreting the Bible: Playing by the Rules*. 2nd ed. Grand Rapids: Baker Academic, 2011.

———. "The 'Criteria' for Authenticity." In *Gospel Perspectives: Studies of History and Tradition in the Four Gospels*, pp. 225-63. Edited by R. T. France and David Wenham. Sheffield: JSOT Press, 1980.

———. "Duality in Mark." In *New Studies in the Synoptic Problem: Oxford Con-

ference, April 2008, pp. 253-80. Edited by P. Foster et al. BETL 239. Leuven: Peeters, 2011.

———. "The Genre of Parables." In *The Challenge of Jesus' Parables*, pp. 30-50. Edited by Richard N. Longenecker. Grand Rapids: Eerdmans, 2000.

———. *Mark*. BECNT. Grand Rapids: Baker Academic, 2008.

———. "A Short Note on Mark XIV.28 and XVI.7." *NTS* 20 (1973): 445-52.

Strauss, David Friedrich. *The Life of Jesus Critically Examined*. Translated by George Eliot. London: Chapman, 1846.

Such, W. A. *The Abomination of Desolation in the Gospel of Mark: Its Historical Reference in Mark 13:14 and Its Impact in the Gospel*. Lanham, MD: University Press of America, 1999.

———. "The Crux Criticorum of Mark 13:14." *Restoration Quarterly* 38 (1996): 93-108.

Taylor, N. H. "Palestinian Christianity and the Caligula Crisis. Part II. The Markan Eschatological Discourse." *JSNT* 62 (1996): 13-41.

Taylor, Vincent. *The Gospel According to St. Mark*. London: Macmillan, 1952.

Theissen, Gerd, and Dagmar Winter. *The Quest for the Plausible Jesus: The Question of Criteria*. Louisville: Westminster John Knox, 2002.

Trocmé, Etienne. *The Formation of the Gospel According to Mark*. Translated by P. Gaughan. Philadelphia: Fortress, 1975.

Victor of Antioch. *The Catena in Marcum: A Byzantine Anthology of Early Commentary on Mark*. Edited by W. R. S. Lamb. TENTS 6. Leiden: Brill, 2012.

Wenham, David. *The Rediscovery of Jesus' Eschatological Discourse*. Gospel Perspectives 4. Sheffield: JSOT Press, 1984.

Wessel, Walter W., and Mark L. Strauss. *Mark*. EBC. Edited by Tremper Longman III and David E. Garland. Grand Rapids: Zondervan, 2010.

Williams, Frank. *The Panarion of Epiphanius of Salamis*. Leiden: Brill. 1987.

Witherington III, Ben. *The Gospel of Mark: A Socio-Rhetorical Commentary*. Grand Rapids: Eerdmans, 2001.

Wrede, William. *The Messianic Secret*. Translated by J. C. G. Greig. Cambridge: James Clarke, 1971.

Wright, N. T. "In Grateful Dialogue: A Response." In *Jesus & the Restoration of Israel: A Critical Assessment of N. T. Wright's Jesus and the Victory of God*, pp. 244-77. Edited by Carey C. Newman. Downers Grove, IL: InterVarsity Press, 1999.

———. *Jesus and the Victory of God*. Minneapolis: Fortress, 1996.

Subject Index

abomination of desolation, 48, 61, 64, 72-76, 79, 85-101, 127, 131
Agrippa II, 82
allegorical interpretation of parables, 132-33
apocalypse, 39, 42-43
Aramaisms, 39-41
Assyrians, 110, 112
audience of Mark, 39-41
author of Mark, 39
author-oriented hermeneutics, 36-41
Babylon, 58, 108-9, 112, 115
Bar Kokhbar, 29
beginning of "birth pangs," 79-80
Caligula, 90
chiasmus, 72-73, 99
coming of the Son of Man, 105-20, 128-30, 132
command to flee Jerusalem, 85-95
constraints on Mark as author, 50-52
cosmic language in prophecy, 107-14
criteria for authenticity (negative)
    contradiction of authentic sayings, 29
    environmental and linguistic contradiction, 28-29
    tendencies of the developing tradition, 28
criteria for authenticity (positive)
    Aramaic linguistic phenomena, 26
    coherence or consistency, 27
    dissimilarity, 24, 26
    double similarity, 32
    embarrassment, 24, 26, 130
    eschatological character, 27
    multiple attestation, 25
    multiple forms, 25-26
    parables and poetry, 27
    tradition contrary to editorial tendency, 26-27
Cross Gospel, 30-32

crux interpreta of Mark 13, 45-46
"D," 34
dating of Mark, 35
divine passive, 26, 28-29, 78
docetism, 24
"E," 34
elect, 98-99
the "end," 78-79, 84-85
false messianic claimants, 76-77, 98-99
farewell discourse, 43
Felix, 82
Festival of Lights. *See* Hanukkah
Festus, 82
The Five Gospels, 30
form criticism, 22
Gallio, 82
Gospel of Peter, 31-32
Gospel of Thomas, 28, 30-31
Hanukkah, 75, 86, 89, 92
Herod, 40
historical narrative, 43, 47
Holy Spirit, 83-84, 102, 110, 112
"in those days," 48, 95-96, 105-7, 120
inclusio, 67, 72, 100
internal-external context, 47-48, 73-76, 93, 100-102
ipsissima verba, 19, 35-37
ipsissima vox, 19, 36-37
"J," 34
Jesus Seminar, 29-32
key for understanding Mark 13, 59-69
"L," 25, 34
Latinisms, 40
"lost tribes of Israel," 110
"M," 25, 34
Marana tha, 98-99, 116-17, 134
Markan restraints in writing, 47, 51-52, 74-75
Markan sandwich, 52
Markan seams, 51
Markan summaries, 51
Medes, 108-9, 112
mirror reading, 47-48, 74-76, 82, 96
Mount of Olives, 54, 60

Nebuchadnezzar, 58, 109, 112
"New Criticism," 37-38
"new quest" for the historical Jesus, 23-32
non-signs of temple's imminent destruction, 76-85
outlines of Mark 13, 43-35
"P," 34
parousia, 79, 83, 96, 103-20, 125, 129-35
Pella, 94-95
Pharaoh Hophra, 109, 112
Pontius Pilate, 40, 90
prophetic perspective, 106-7, 120
Proto-Luke, 34
Proto-Mark, 34
"Q," 25, 34
quest for the historical Jesus, 19-23
reader-response hermeneutics, 38
readers of Mark, 39-41, 86-87
redaction criticism, 37
Samaria, 110, 112
Secret Gospel of Mark, 30-31
Semitic redundancy, 97-98
Sitz im Leben, 37, 47, 77, 100-102
Son of God, 131
source analysis of Mark, 33-36
step parallelism, 36, 45-46, 63
synonymous parallelism, 36, 45, 62-63, 68
temple
    contemporary prophecies of its destruction, 57-58
    magnificence of, 55-56
"these things" and "all these things," 45-46, 48, 50, 61-69, 100, 121-22, 124, 125-27, 128-29
"third quest" for the historical Jesus, 32-33
"this generation," 125-26
Titus, 58-59, 90
Traditionsgeschichte, 60
Wolfenbüttel Fragments, 19
Zealots, 90, 92-93

Author Index

Adams, E., 63, 116, 124, 126
Allison, D. C., 107
Ambrozic, A. M., 104
Aune, D. E., 43
Bahat, D., 55
Balabanski, V., 94
Barnes, T. D., 55
Beasley-Murray, G. R., 17, 37, 44, 56, 58, 62, 64, 68, 75, 77, 78, 79, 80, 89, 95, 96, 97, 106, 112, 113, 130, 132
Beavis, M. A., 118
Bengel, J. A., 62, 106
Bird, M. F., 40
Black, C. C., 43
Bock, D. L., 110
Boring, M. E., 63, 112
Bornkamm, G., 22, 25
Brooks, J. A., 44, 62
Brown, C., 19
Bultmann, R., 24, 130
Caird, G. B., 107
Chanikuzhy, J., 53-53
Charlesworth, J. H., 84
Collins, A. Y., 43, 44, 59, 61, 62, 77, 78, 85, 86, 104
Collins, A. Y., and J. C. Collins, 117
Coloni, T., 34-35
Cranfield, C. E. B., 66, 91, 124, 126
Davies, W. D., and D. C. Allison, 63
Dean, J. D., 94
Deppe, D. B., 72-73
Dilthy, W., 23
Donahue, J. R., 57
Donahue, J. R., and D. J. Harrington, 44, 63, 78
Edwards, J. R., 44, 59, 91, 95, 128
Ernst, J., 62
Evans, C. A., 31, 32, 44, 46, 53, 58, 59, 62, 71, 77, 82, 86, 91, 95, 97, 120, 126, 128
Focant, C., 44, 63, 104, 105, 113, 123, 128

Ford, D., 90
Fowler, R. M., 86
France, R. T., 45, 50, 53, 63, 69, 78, 80, 83, 91, 95, 98, 118, 125, 126, 128, 129, 131
Funk, R. W., and Roy W. Hoover, 30
Gaston, L., 63, 90
Geddert, T. J., 61
Gibbs, J. A., 129
Gnilka, J., 104
Gould, E. P., 44, 90
Gray, T. C., 80, 87, 104, 105
Grayston, K., 17, 35, 72
Grundmann, W., 21
Gumerlock, F. X., 130
Gundry, R. H., 44, 50, 71, 72, 87, 101, 124
Hare, D. R. A., 81
Hatina, T. R., 44
Hendriksen, W., 44, 62, 106
Hengel, M., 32, 38, 74, 86
Hooker, M. D., 40, 43, 44, 62, 67, 82, 85, 86, 90, 128, 129
Hurtado, L. W., 43, 58, 71, 76, 124
Jeremias, J., 124
Kähler, M., 21
Käsemann, E., 24-25
Kelber, W. H., 62, 93
Lambrecht, J., 72
Lane, W. L., 43, 63, 64, 86, 94, 97, 99, 104, 123, 125, 128
Lightfoot, R. H., 74
Lohmeyer, E., 74
Lührmann, D., 90
Manson, T. W., 90
Marcus, J., 43, 44, 51, 63, 78, 80, 82, 90, 92, 99, 120, 123, 125, 128, 135
Martin, T. W., 134
Marxsen, W., 74
McKenna, M., 71
McKnight, S., 44, 116
Meier, J. P., 32, 130
Merkle, B. L., 81

Moloney, F. J., 43, 44, 61, 72, 87, 90, 93, 94
Neill, E., and N. T. Wright, 32
Nineham, D. E., 44
Painter, J., 62
Paulus, H. E. G., 20
Perkins, L., 87
Pesch, R., 44, 61, 62, 91, 94, 96, 104
Pitre, B., 86
Polhill, J. B., 110
Porter, S. E., 29
Reimarus, H. S., 19
Robinson, J. M., 23-24
Sanders, E. P., 28
Schnabel, E., 85, 104
Schweitzer, A., 19, 22, 23
Snodgrass, K. R., 27
Snow, R. S., 92
Sowers, S., 94
Stein, R. H., 15, 29, 35, 38, 39, 40, 51, 59, 74, 76, 78, 79, 82, 97, 123, 133
Strauss, D. F., 20
Such, W. A., 69, 90
Taylor, N. H., 90
Taylor, V., 40, 44, 82, 84, 91, 130
Theissen, G., and D. Winter, 26, 29
Tindal, M., 19
Toland, J., 19
Trocmé, E., 76
Tyrell, G., 22
Victor of Antioch, 46, 72
Von Ranke, L., 23
Wenham, D., 35
Wessel, W. W., and M. L. Strauss, 44, 63
Williams, F., 94
Witherington, B., III, 43, 78, 90, 92, 104, 121, 126
Woolston, T., 19
Wrede, W., 21
Wright, N. T., 23, 32, 44, 69, 114, 115, 116

Mark Index

1:1, *54, 82*
1:1–8:21, *50-51*
1:4, *26, 50*
1:4-8, *39*
1:5, *93*
1:9, *26, 95, 106, 120*
1:14, *51*
1:14-15, *50, 82*
1:14–3:6, *50*
1:14–8:21, *50*
1:16, *51*
1:16-18, *60*
1:16-20, *50*
1:19-20, *60*
1:21, *51*
1:21-45, *52*
1:29-31, *60*
1:32, *54*
1:34, *86*
1:39, *51*
1:40-45, *60*
1:44, *82*
2:1, *51*
2:1–3:6, *52*
2:4, *40*
2:9, *40*
2:10, *86*
2:11, *40*
2:13, *51*
2:19-20, *97*
3:4, *97*
3:6, *50, 54*
3:7, *51, 93*
3:7-12, *50-51*
3:7–6:6a, *50*
3:8, *83*
3:13-19, *50*
3:16-20, *60*
3:17, *74*
3:17-22, *39*
3:22, *74*
3:28, *125*
3:30, *86*
3:32, *60*
4:1, *51, 60*
4:1-34, *52*
4:9, *86*
4:10, *60, 71*
4:11-34, *71*
4:17, *80*
4:21, *40*
4:23, *86*
4:24, *76*

4:25, *26*
4:30, *97*
4:34, *60*
4:35, *51, 54, 95, 106, 120*
4:35-41, *60*
4:35–5:43, *52*
5:1, *51, 54*
5:1-20, *83*
5:2, *54*
5:2–6:1, *54*
5:6, *54*
5:7, *54*
5:8, *54*
5:9, *40, 54*
5:10, *54*
5:12, *54*
5:13, *54*
5:15, *40, 54*
5:17, *54*
5:18, *54*
5:19, *54*
5:20, *54*
5:21, *51, 54*
5:22, *54*
5:23, *54, 97*
5:24, *54*
5:27, *54*
5:28, *54*
5:30, *54*
5:31, *54*
5:32, *54*
5:33, *54*
5:34, *54*
5:35, *54*
5:36, *54*
5:37, *54, 60*
5:38, *54*
5:39, *54*
5:40, *54*
5:40-43, *60*
5:41, *19, 39, 54, 74*
5:43, *54*
6:1, *51, 54*
6:1-6a, *50*
6:2, *54*
6:6b, *50*
6:6b–8:21, *50*
6:7-13, *50, 60*
6:11, *82*
6:14, *51*
6:17-29, *29*
6:27, *40*
6:30-32, *60*

6:31, *60*
6:32, *60*
6:32-34, *51*
6:33-37, *60*
6:37, *40*
6:45, *51*
6:45-52, *60*
6:48, *40, 134*
6:53, *51*
6:54, *54*
6:55, *40*
7:3, *40*
7:3-4, *40*
7:4, *40*
7:11, *19, 39, 74, 86*
7:13, *97*
7:17, *71*
7:18, *68*
7:18-23, *71*
7:19, *86*
7:23, *68*
7:24, *51*
7:24-30, *60*
7:24-31, *83*
7:31, *51*
7:33, *60*
7:34, *19, 39*
8:1, *54, 95, 106, 120*
8:10, *51*
8:11-12, *61*
8:12, *125*
8:14-21, *50, 60*
8:15, *76*
8:17-18, *68*
8:18, *86*
8:22, *50-51*
8:22–10:52, *50-51*
8:27, *51*
8:27-33, *60*
8:34-38, *17-18, 28, 47, 80, 101, 137*
8:35, *81-82, 84*
8:36, *113*
8:38, *84, 98, 113, 116-18, 125*
9:1, *125*
9:2, *60*
9:2-13, *60*
9:9, *54*
9:19, *68, 125*
9:28, *60, 71*
9:29, *71*
9:30, *51*

9:30-32, *51, 60*
9:33, *51*
9:33-37, *60*
9:38, *71*
9:38-41, *60*
9:39-41, *71*
9:41, *125*
9:42-50, *60*
9:43, *39, 74*
10:1, *51, 93*
10:10-11, *60*
10:11-12, *28*
10:12, *29*
10:13, *71*
10:14-16, *71*
10:15, *125*
10:17, *54, 81*
10:17-31, *60*
10:20, *68*
10:29, *82, 125*
10:30, *80*
10:32, *51*
10:32-34, *51*
10:32-45, *60*
10:35, *71*
10:36-40, *71*
10:40, *26*
10:46, *39, 51, 54, 74*
11:1, *51, 55*
11:1-19, *42*
11:1-26, *68*
11:1-12:44, *54*
11:1-13:37, *42*
11:1-16:8, *50-51*
11:11, *51-52, 55*
11:11-12, *51, 60*
11:11-14, *60, 123*
11:11-19, *53*
11:12, *51, 54-55*
11:12-14, *52, 60, 122*
11:12-25, *42, 55*
11:13, *122*
11:15, *51-52*
11:15-17, *88*
11:15-19, *52, 122*
11:17, *83*
11:17-18, *52*
11:18, *54*
11:19, *55*
11:20, *55*
11:20-21, *122-23*
11:20-25, *52, 60*
11:23, *125*

11:27, *51, 54-55*
11:27-33, *42*, 52
11:28, *68*, 97
11:30, *26*
12:1, *54*
12:1-12, *42, 53, 55*, 88
12:6, *131*
12:9, *53*
12:10-11, *40*
12:12, *53-54*
12:13-17, *42*
12:13-37, *52*
12:14, *40*, 97
12:15, *40*
12:18-27, *42*
12:23, 97
12:26, *40*
12:28-34, *52*
12:34, *52*
12:35, *51*
12:37, *54*
12:38-40, *42*
12:41, *51*, 60
12:41-44, *60*
12:42, *40*
12:43, *54, 125*
13:1, *51*, **54-55**, *59-60, 69*, 129
13:1-2, *42, 59-60, 66*
13:1-4, *49-50, 59, 69*, 129
13:1-5a, *93*
13:1-7, *79*
13:1-23, *42, 80, 100*, 119-21
13:1-31, *45*
13:1-37, *44, 49, 52, 54*, 66-67
13:2, *17, 30, 46, 54-55*, **56-59**, *60-61, 63-65, 69, 72, 75, 77, 80, 83*, 97, 100, 105, 118, 124, 126
13:2-3, *46*
13:3, *46, 51, 54, 59-60, 69*
13:3-4, **59-69**, *105*
13:3-13, *59*
13:3-23, *126*
13:3-37, *59-60*
13:4, *17, 36, 45-46, 48, 54, 59-61, 63-69, 71-72, 75, 77-80, 83, 85*, 97, 100, 104-5, 112, 115, 118, 121-22, 124-27, 129, 130, 134
13:5, *64, 67, 71, 73, 76, 79-80, 98*, 100, 104, 118, 124, 129-30, 134
13:5-6, *72-73*, **76-77**, *79*, 99

13:5-7, *69*
13:5-8, *35*, 135
13:5-13, *44, 69, 73*, **76-85**, *86*
13:5-16, *120*
13:5-23, *42-44, 46, 48-49, 55, 61, 63-64, 67, 71-74, 76, 79, 80, 83*, 100, 104-7, 114-15, 118-20, 122, 124, 126-27, 129, 134
13:5-24, *129*
13:5-37, *18, 33, 45-46, 52, 59, 60-61, 64, 98*
13:6, *18, 35, 48*
13:6-7, *79*
13:7, *35, 69, 71, 73, 77-79, 84-85*, 105, 134
13:7-8, *35, 46, 72-73*, **77-80**
13:7-12, *47*
13:7-20, *99*
13:8, *35, 71, 78-79*
13:8-13, *69*
13:9, *46, 64, 71, 73, 76, 80-84*, 105, 119, 134
13:9-13, *72-73, 79*, **80-85**
13:10, *18, 63, 72, 78, 82-83*, 101
13:11, *35, 37, 46-47, 72-73, 78, 81-83, 85*, 105, 134
13:12, *35, 79*
13:12-16, *35*
13:13, *48, 79, 81-82, 84*, 105, 134
13:13b-20, *35*
13:14, *18, 35, 46, 48, 61, 63-65, 69, 72, 76, 80, 85-90, 92-93, 97*, 105, 112, 124, 127, 129, 134
13:14-16, *46, 64, 86, 94-95*
13:14-18, *97*
13:14-20, *35, 72-73, 75-76*, **85-98**
13:14-22, *35*
13:14-23, *18, 47, 93*, 106
13:14-27, *44*
13:15, *95*
13:15-16, *91*
13:15-23, *69*, 104
13:16, *95*
13:16-17, *93*
13:17, *64*, 105, 120, 129, *131*
13:17-20, *95*
13:18, *35, 64, 73, 92*, 105, *134*

13:19, *48, 63, 96-97*, 119-20, 125, 129, 131
13:19-20, *96-97*, 105
13:19-22, *35*
13:20, *97-98*, 101, 129, *131*
13:21, *30, 46, 72-73*, 104-5, *134*
13:21-22, *77, 98-99*
13:21-23, *46, 72-73*, **98-100**, *135*
13:22, *35, 63, 98*
13:23, *64, 67, 71, 73, 76, 79-80*, 100, 104-5, 118, 124, 134
13:24, *18, 48, 67, 72, 97*, **103-7**, *119-20, 129-31*
13:24b-25, *103*, **107-12**, *114, 116, 119*
13:24-27, *18, 34-35, 42-44, 48-49, 62-64, 67, 72, 79, 83, 97*, 104-6, 113-15, 118-20, 122-24, 126-27, *129*, 131, 134
13:24-37, *44*
13:26, *98*, 105, 112, 123, *130, 133*
13:26-27, *103*, **113-18**
13:27, *98, 119*, 130
13:28, *73*, 105, 129
13:28-29, *30, 61, 121*, **122-24**
13:28-30, *126, 128, 134*
13:28-31, *42-44, 48-49, 55*, 105, 121-23, **125-27**, *127-30, 134*
13:28-37, *44*
13:29, *48, 64-65, 73*, 105, 121-24, *127*
13:29-30, *50, 121*, 125-26, 129-30
13:30, *18, 46, 48, 64-65, 68-69, 75*, 100, 105, 115, 121-22, 124-27, 130, 136
13:30-31, **125-27**, *129*
13:31, *28, 47, 121-22*, 125-26
13:32, *26, 30, 60*, 105-6, 128-30, *133*
13:32-33, **130-32**
13:32-37, *42-45, 48-49, 63, 79, 83*, 105, 120, 122, *134*
13:33, *64, 73, 76*, 105, 129-32, *134*
13:33-37, *48, 122*, 128-29
13:34, **132-33**

13:34-35, *131*
13:34-36, *30*, 130
13:35, *40, 73*, 105-6, 129-30, 133-34
13:35-36, **133-34**
13:36, *105*, 134
13:37, *42, 73*, 105, 130, *133*, **134-35**
14:1, *42, 51, 54, 56, 60*
14:1-2, *42, 54*
14:3, *51, 54*
14:3-9, *60*
14:5, *40*
14:8-9, *42*
14:9, *82-83*, 125
14:10-11, *42*
14:12, *51, 74*, 123
14:12-42, *60*
14:17, *54*, 134
14:18, *125*
14:22, *54*
14:23-25, *42*
14:25, *85*, 125
14:27-28, *42*
14:28, *74*
14:30, *125*
14:31, *125*
14:32, *51*
14:33, *60*
14:35, *99*
14:36, *19, 39, 74*
14:37, *68*, 134
14:38, *132*
14:43, *51, 54*
14:49, *40*
14:53, *51*
14:58, *42, 57-58*
14:61-62, *26*
14:62, *42*, 116, 118
14:72, *134*
15:1, *51*, 134
15:15, *40*
15:16, *40*, 51
15:21, *39, 47, 51*
15:22, *39, 74*
15:29, *42, 57-58*
15:30-31, *97*
15:33, *54*
15:34, *19, 39, 74*
15:38, *42*
15:39, *40, 42*
15:42, *74*, 134
15:44, *40*
15:45, *40*
16:1, *54*
16:1-6, *42*
16:7, *74*

Scripture Index

OLD TESTAMENT

Genesis
8:22, *126*
37:19, *135*

Exodus
3:12, *61*
4:10-17, *83*
7:8-13, *61*
9:18, *96*
11:6, *96*

Deuteronomy
4:32, *96*

Judges
4, *111*
5:4-5, *111*
7:19, *134*

2 Samuel
17:13, *59*

2 Kings
8:12, *95*
15:16, *95*
19:29, *61*
25:9, *56*

2 Chronicles
15:6, *78*
36:15-21, *62*
36:19, *56*

Nehemiah
2:11-17, *62*

Psalms
18:7 9, *111*
48:8-9, *94*
48:12-14, *94*
74:3-7, *35*
77:18, *111*
82:5, *111*
96, *83*
102:25-27, *126*
105:6, *98*
110:1, *118*
137:1-9, *35*

Isaiah
2:11-12, *131*
2:11-22, *131*
2:20, *131*
3:11, *95*
5:1-7, *53*
5:7, *53*
7:11-17, *61*
11:11-12, *119*
13, *109*
13:1-22, *108*
13:3, *109*
13:8, *80*
13:9-11, *18, 108, 112*
13:10, *115*
13:11, *109, 115*
13:12, *109*
13:13, *109*
19:2, *78, 84*
21:3, *80*
26:17, *80*
27:12-13, *119*
28:1, *95*
29:1, *95*
29:15, *95*
30:1, *95*
31:1, *95*
33:1, *95*
34:8, *131*
35:1-10, *119*
40, *126*
40:3-5, *111*
42:1, *98*
42:6-7, *83*
43:5-13, *119*
43:20, *98*
49:6, *83*
49:12, *83*
49:22, *119*
51:6, *126*
52:10, *83*
54:9-10, *126*
56:1-8, *83*
60:1-9, *119*
60:1-16, *83*
60:21-22, *98*
65:9, *98*
65:15, *98*
66:20, *119*

Jeremiah
1:6-10, *83*
3:16, *105, 120*
3:18, *105, 120*
4:12, *109*
4:13, *95*
4:16-31, *62*
4:23-24, *115*
4:23-26, *108*
4:23-27, *112*
4:23-28, *18*
4:25-26, *115*
4:31, *80*
5:18, *105*
5:18-19, *120*
5:19, *109*
6:1, *94*
6:13, *99*
6:19, *109*
6:24, *80*
7, *92*
7:13-20, *56*
7:14, *35*
9:11, *35*
9:19-22, *62*
12:7-13, *62*
13:27, *95*
14:14, *99*
15:1-9, *62*
21:1-10, *62*
22:23, *80*
23:7-8, *119*
23:32, *99*
25:11-14, *62*
26:6, *35, 56*
26:9, *56*
26:17-18, *56*
26:17-19, *35*
27:1-22, *62*
30:6, *80*
31:10-14, *119*
31:29, *105*
31:29-30, *120*
32:24-29, *35*
33:14-16, *120*
33:15-16, *105*
33:20-21, *127*
39:1-10, *62*
46:10, *131*
50:4, *105*
50:43, *80*
51:24-58, *78*
52:1-30, *62*
52:4-30, *35*

Lamentations
1–2, *62*
2:7-9, *56*

Ezekiel
4–5, *62*
4:1-3, *35*
7:7-27, *131*
8–9, *88, 89*
8:6, *88*
11:22-25, *60*
13:5, *131*
13:18, *95*
32:5-8, *18*
32:7-8, *109, 112, 115*
32:9-10, *115*
38:21, *84*
39:25-29, *119*

Daniel
7–12, *42*
7:13, *118*
9:25-27, *91*
9:26, *56*
9:27, *75, 87, 88*
11–12, *89*
11:29-35, *91*
11:31, *56, 75, 87, 88, 89*
12:1, *42, 96*
12:1-13, *91*
12:5-13, *87*
12:11, *75, 88*

Hosea
7:13, *95*
9:12, *95*
13:13, *80*
13:16, *95*

Joel
2:1-2, *96, 129*
2:28-32, *110, 111*
2:29, *105, 120*
2:30-32, *112*
2:32, *129*
3:1, *105*
3:14, *129*
3:18, *129, 131*

Amos
1:13, *95*
5:18, *95*
5:18-20, *131*
8:3, *131*
8:9, *115, 131*
8:9-10, *109, 112*
8:10-11, *115*

8:13, *131*
9:5, *111*
9:11, *131*

Micah
1:4, *111*
3:9-12, *35*
3:12, *56*
4:6, *131*
4:9-10, *80*
5:10, *131*
6:8, *52*
7:6, *84*
7:12, *131*

Nahum
1:5, *111*

Habakkuk
3:6, *111*

Zephaniah
1:7-18, *131*
3:16, *131*

Haggai
2:15, *59*

Zechariah
2, *120*
8:23, *105, 120*
9:16, *131*
10:6-12, *119*
13:2, *99*
14:1-21, *131*
14:2, *62*
14:4-5, *60*

NEW TESTAMENT

Matthew
1–2, *89*
3:1, *95, 106, 120*
3:13-17, *26*
4:9, *68*
5:1, *60*
5:18, *126*
5:22, *19*
5:29, *19*
5:34-35, *26*
6:9, *26*
6:9-13, *99*
6:10, *98, 134*
6:24, *19*
6:32, *68*
6:33, *68*
7:1, *26*
7:7, *26*
7:15-20, *99*
7:22-23, *76*
7:28-29, *67*
10:17, *81*
10:21, *84*
10:30, *26*
10:34-39, *84*
11:1, *67*
11:13, *27*
11:15, *86*
11:16, *125*
11:27, *131*
12:41, *125*
12:42, *125*
12:45, *125*
13:9, *86*
13:15, *86*
13:34, *68*
13:34-35, *67*
13:36-43, *113*
13:40-42, *117*
13:51, *68*
13:56, *68*
16:27, *113*
16:27-28, *117*
19:1, *67*
19:20, *68*
19:28, *113*
21:43, *53*
22:8-10, *53*
23:4, *88*
23:23, *88*
23:23-24, *52*
23:25-28, *88*
23:29-39, *52*
23:36, *68, 125*
23:37, *88*
23:37-39, *55*
23:38, *57*
24, *85*
24–25, *30*
24:1-36, *67*
24:1-44, *52*
24:1-51, *18*
24:2, *68*
24:3, *66, 67, 69*
24:5, *77*
24:8, *68*
24:15, *86*
24:21, *104*
24:30, *98*
24:33, *68*
24:34, *68, 125*
24:36, *129*
24:36-44, *113*
24:37–25:46, *66, 67*
24:40-41, *81*
24:42-44, *99*
24:43-44, *132*
24:45-51, *67, 113, 132*
25:1-13, *113*
25:1-46, *18*
25:14-28, *30*
25:14-30, *67, 113, 132, 134*
25:31, *117*
25:31-46, *113*
26:1, *67*
26:55, *60*
26:64, *118*
28:19-20, *83*

Mark
See Mark Index, p. 151

Luke
1–2, *89*
1:1-2, *75*
1:1-4, *65*
1:2, *28, 118*
1:4, *74*
1:52, *111*
1:65, *68*
2:1, *95, 106, 120*
2:19, *68*
3:4-6, *111*
4:2, *95, 106, 120*
4:20-21, *60*
5:3, *60*
5:35, *95, 106, 120*
6:35, *26*
7:31, *125*
8:8, *86*
9:26, *117*
9:36, *95, 106, 120*
9:44, *86*
10:22, *131*
11:2, *98, 134*
11:2-4, *99*
11:29, *125*
11:30, *125*
11:31, *125*
11:32, *125*
11:50, *125*
11:51, *125*
12:8-9, *26, 113*
12:30, *68*
12:35-38, *132*
12:36-40, *134*
12:39-40, *99, 132*
12:42-46, *67, 132*
12:52-53, *84*
13:31-35, *55*
13:34, *88*
13:35, *57*
14:11, *111*
14:35, *86*
15:10, *26*
15:21, *26*
16:14, *68*
16:17, *126*
17:22-24, *98*
17:25, *125*
17:34-35, *81*
18:14, *111*
18:21, *68*
19:12-27, *67, 132, 134*
19:43-44, *57*
21:5-6, *66*
21:5-36, *18*
21:6, *65*
21:7, *66, 69*
21:32, *125*
21:36, *68*
24:9, *68*

John
2, *52*
2:13-22, *52*
2:19, *57*
3:16-17, *131*
3:35, *131*
3:36, *131*
5:25-29, *113*
8:2, *60*
10:3, *133*
10:22, *89*
10:22-23, *75*
13–21, *43*
15:18-19, *84*
15:21, *68*
21:22-23, *117*
21:25, *118*

Acts
1:9, *116*
1:11, *116*
2:6-11, *110*
2:14-16, *110*
2:14-17, *84*
2:16-21, *110, 112*
2:17-18, *111*
2:17-21, *112*
2:18, *115*
2:19-20, *111, 115*
2:21, *111, 115*
2:33, *118*
4:1-22, *81*
4:8, *83, 84*
4:13, *83*
4:31, *84*
5:17-18, *81*
5:27-42, *81*
5:31, *118*
5:37, *77*

Scripture Index

6:3–7:60, *81*
6:8-10, *84*
6:8–7:60, *81*
6:14, *57*
7:50, *68*
7:55, *84*
8:1-3, *81*
8:1-24, *76*
8:29-35, *84*
9:1-2, *81*
9:13-16, *81*
9:23-24, *81*
11:26, *84*
12:1-5, *81*
12:4, *134*
12:12, *39*
13:9-10, *84*
13:44-47, *53*
14:18, *81*
15:31, *87*
16:19-40, *81*
17:16, *118*
17:19-31, *118*
17:31, *113*
18:12-17, *81, 82*
19:13-16, *76*
19:13-17, *76*
22:19, *81*
22:30–23:10, *81*
23:23–24:27, *82*
24:1-27, *81*
24:27–26:32, *82*
25:1-12, *81*
25:13–26:32, *82*
28:30-31, *92*

Romans
1:5, *83*
1:8, *83*
6:17, *75*
7:7-25, *24*
8:28, *82*
8:33, *98*
9:11-16, *53*
10:18, *83*

10:19, *53*
15:19, *83*
15:23, *83*
16:26, *18, 83*

1 Corinthians
1:26, *84*
4:5, *113*
7:1, *129*
7:25, *129*
8:1, *129*
11:23, *74*
11:23-26, *74*
12:1, *129*
12:11, *68*
15:23, *116*
16:1, *129*
16:12, *129*
16:22, *98, 99, 134*

2 Corinthians
1:13, *87*
5:16, *23*
11:3, *76*
11:24-25, *81*

Galatians
1:7, *76*
2:4, *76*
6:12, *76*

Ephesians
3:4, *87*

Philippians
3:17-19, *76*

Colossians
1:6, *18, 83*
1:23, *18*
1:26, *83*
3:12, *98*
4:16, *87*

1 Thessalonians
4:9, *129*

4:13-18, *98*
4:15, *116*
4:15-17, *116*
4:16-17, *117*
4:17, *135*
4:18, *134*
5:1, *129*
5:2, *99, 117, 131*
5:4, *117, 131*
5:11, *134*

2 Thessalonians
1:5-10, *113*

2:1, *116*
2:2, *77, 131*
2:3, *131*
2:3-4, *91*
2:8-10, *113*
2:8-12, *99*

1 Timothy
4:1, *77*

2 Timothy
2:10, *98*
4:1, *113*
4:8, *134*

Titus
1:1, *98*
1:10, *77*
2:13, *98, 116, 119, 134*

Hebrews
1:1-9, *131*
1:10-12, *126*

1 Peter
1:1, *98*
2:9-10, *53*
4:14-16, *82*

2 Peter
1:10, *99*

2:1-3, *77*
3:3-4, *135*
3:4, *116*
3:7, *126*
3:10, *99, 113, 126*

1 John
2:18, *99*
4:1, *99*
4:1-6, *77*

2 John
7, *77*

Jude
8, *135*
14–15, *113*

Revelation
1:1, *43*
1:3, *43, 86*
2:2, *77*
2:7, *86*
2:11, *86*
2:17, *86*
2:29, *86*
3:3, *99*
3:6, *86*
3:13, *86*
3:22, *86*
6:14, *126*
7:14, *104*
13:9, *86*
16:15, *99*
16:18, *96*
17:14, *98*
18:4, *94*
19:1-21, *113*
20:11, *126*
21:1, *126*
22:7, *43*
22:10, *43*
22:18-19, *43*
22:20, *98, 117, 134*

Ancient Writings Index

APOCRYPHA
Baruch
4:1, *126*
5:5-9, *119*

2 Esdras
2:13, *98*
4:51, *120*
4:52, *61*
6:25, *85*
9:1-6, *78*
9:36-37, *126*
13, *42*
13:29-32, *78*

1 Maccabees
1:20–4:61, *87*
1:41-64, *89, 91*
1:47, *89, 91*
1:54, *75, 89*
1:59, *75, 89*
2:27-28, *94*
4:36-59, *89*
4:56, *89*
4:59, *89*
6:7, *89*
9:27, *96*

2 Maccabees
1:9, *89*
1:18, *89*
2:9, *89*
2:16, *89*
2:18, *89*
2:19, *89*
6:1–10:8, *87*
6:5, *89*
10:3, *89*
10:5, *89*
14:33, *56*

Sirach
36:10, *98*

Tobit
13:13, *119*
14:4, *56*

Wisdom
18:4, *126*

PSEUDEPIGRAPHA
Apocalypse of Baruch
70:2-8, *78*

Assumption of Moses
8:1, *96*

2 Baruch
20:1, *98*
25:1-4, *61*
54:1, *98*
83:1, *98*

1 Enoch
37–71, *42*
80:2, *98*
90:28, *56*
99:4, *78*

Joseph and Asenath
11:4-6, *85*

Jubilees
11:2, *78*
49:10-12, *134*

Psalms of Solomon
11:1-9, *119*

Sibylline Oracles
3:63-69, *99*
3:635-36, *78*

Testament of Judah
22:1, *78*

Testament of Naphtali
5:1, *60*

JOSEPHUS
Antiquities
2.325, *89*
5.223, *134*
12.254, *89*
15.392, *55*
15.396, *55*
17.271, *77*
17.273-77, *77*
17.278-84, *77*
18.55-59, *90*

18.261-309, *90*
18.356, *134*
20.169-72, *60*

Jewish War
1.34, *89*
2:56, *77*
2.57-59, *77*
2.60-65, *77*
2.169-74, *70*
2.433-44, *99*
2.433-48, *77, 99*
2.585-89, *77*
4.106-11, *94*
4.121-25, *94*
4.121-27, *77*
4.135-37, *94*
4.147-57, *90*
4.151-57, *93*
4.160, *90*
4.503-44, *77, 99*
4:510, *99*
4.566-83, *77*
5.510-11, *134*
5.222-23, *55*
5.224, *55*
6.249-87, *35*
6.260, *90*
6.281-87, *77*
6.285-88, *99*
6.285-300, *99*
6.301, *57*
6.306, *57*
6.309, *57*
6.316, *90*
6.352-55, *59*
6.363-64, *59*
6.409-13, *59*
7.1-4, *59*

NEW TESTAMENT APOCRYPHA
Gospel of Thomas
47, *28*

RABBINIC WRITINGS
Babylonian Talmud
Baba Meṣiʻa, 85b, *98*
Baba Qamma 6.6, *89*

Berakot 3b, *134*
Sukkah 51b, *55*

Mishnah
Berakot 1.1, *134*

DEAD SEA SCROLLS
1QM 1.11-12, *96*

PAPYRI
Oxyrhynchus
2949, *32*
4009, *32*

CLASSICAL WRITINGS
Tacitus
Fragments of the Histories 2, *55*

Epiphanius
Panarion or *Refutation of Heresies*
29.7.7-8, *94*
30.2.7, *94*
Treatise on Weights and Measures
15, *94*

CHURCH FATHERS
Didache
16:4, *77*

Epistle of Barnabus
4:3, *98*

Eusebius
Ecclesiastical History
3.5.3 (3.114-15), *94*

Tertullian
Apology 50, *82*

Victor of Antioch
The Catena in Marcum
Mark 13:14, *46, 62*

Finding the Textbook You Need

The IVP Academic Textbook Selector
is an online tool for instantly finding the IVP books
suitable for over 250 courses across 24 disciplines.

ivpacademic.com

www.ingramcontent.com/pod-product-compliance
Lightning Source LLC
Chambersburg PA
CBHW031434150426
43191CB00006B/519